THE INTERNET COMPANION

A Beginner's Guide to Global Networking

TRACY LAQUEY
with Jeanne C. Ryer

Foreword by Vice President Al Gore

AN EDITORIAL INC. BOOK

Addison-Wesley Publishing Company
Reading, Massachusetts ▪ Menlo Park, California ▪ New York
Don Mills, Ontario ▪ Wokingham, England ▪ Amsterdam
Bonn ▪ Sydney ▪ Singapore ▪ Tokyo ▪ Madrid ▪ San Juan
Paris ▪ Seoul ▪ Milan ▪ Mexico City ▪ Taipei

Many of the designations used by manufacturers and sellers to distinguish their products are claimed as trademarks. Where those designations appear in this book, and Addison-Wesley was aware of a trademark claim, the designations have been printed in initial capital letters or all capital letters.

The authors and publishers have taken care in preparation of this book, but make no expressed or implied warranty of any kind and assume no responsibility for errors or omissions. No liability is assumed for incidental or consequential damages in connection with or arising out of the use of the information or programs contained herein.

Library of Congress Cataloging-in-Publication Data
LaQuey, Tracy 1963-
    The Internet companion: a beginner's guide to global networking/
Tracy LaQuey with Jeanne C. Ryer.
        p.   cm.
    Includes index.
    ISBN 0-201-62224-6
    1. Internet (Computer network) I. Ryer, Jeanne C. II. Title.
TK5105.875.I57L37 1992
384.3--dc20
                                                            92-31691
                                                                CIP

Sponsoring Editor: Keith Wollman
Project Editor: Elizabeth Rogalin
Cover and text design: Arisman Design
Illustrations: Steven Ackerman
Set in Meridien and Futura type by Editorial Inc.

5 6 7 8 9–MW–96959493
Fifth printing, April 1993

Contents

Chapter 4

Finding Information   75

Chapter 5

Internet In-the-Know Guide   109

Chapter 6

Getting Connected   139

Foreword

Computer networks have been around for over twenty-five years, and in that time they have gone from being a laboratory curiosity to a tool used by millions of people every day. The first network, ARPANET, was used primarily by a few thousand computer scientists to access computers, share computer files, and send electronic mail. Today, scientists, engineers, teachers, students, librarians, doctors, businesspeople, and even a few members of Congress rely on the Internet and other networks to communicate with their colleagues, receive electronic journals, access bulletin boards, log onto databases, and use remote computers and other equipment.

In the last few years, we have witnessed the democratization of the Internet. Today, the network connects not only the top research laboratories and universities but also small colleges, small businesses, libraries, and high schools throughout the country. The growth of commercial networks has enabled much broader access to the government-subsidized portions of the Internet. And that growth is accelerating because the telecommunications and computer industries have recognized the commercial potential of high-speed, packet-switched networking and have invested hundreds of millions of dollars in developing new switching technology and new applications for networks.

Since I first became interested in high-speed networking almost fifteen years ago, there have been many major advances both in the technology and in public awareness.

Articles on high-speed networks are commonplace in major newspapers and in news magazines. In contrast, when as a House member in the early 1980s I called for creation of a national network of "information superhighways," the only people interested were the manufacturers of optical fiber. Back then, of course, high speed meant 56,000 bits per second. Today we are building the National Research and Education Network, which will carry billions of bits of data per second, serve thousands of users simultaneously, and transmit not only electronic mail and data files but voice and video as well.

Unfortunately, it is not easy to keep track of all the new developments in networking. According to some recent estimates, the amount of traffic on the Internet has been increasing 10 percent per month, and the number of new applications and services has been growing almost as quickly. You can now access thousands of different databases and bulletin boards on everything from medieval French literature to global warming. Since the Internet is a network of networks, there is no one place to go for information on what's available and how to access it. Most users have had to rely on friends and colleagues for information on the Internet.

That is why I welcome publication of *The Internet Companion*. It provides a valuable primer on the Internet, explains the "rules of the road," and provides step-by-step instructions on accessing many of the information resources available through the Internet. It should help both new and experienced Internet users learn how to make the best use of the network.

For too many people the Internet has been uncharted territory, and as a result they have hesitated to explore the vast potential of networking. I trust this book will change that.

August 1992   Al Gore

Preface

If you want to stay current in the nineties, and even into the next century, you need to learn about the Internet. Futurists predict that information and access to it will be the basis for personal, business, and political advancement in the next century. Whether you want to find the latest financial news, browse through library catalogs, trace your genealogy, exchange information with your colleagues, or join in lively political debate, the Internet is the tool that will take you beyond phones, faxes, and isolated computers to the real electronic information frontier. The Internet can shrink the world and bring knowledge, experience, and information on nearly every subject imaginable straight to your computer. It can give you the power and speed of a supercomputer, even if you have only a microcomputer and a modem.

The Internet Companion is an introduction to this vast electronic wonderland. We will tell you why you need to know about the Internet and show you how people are already using it in their everyday activities. We'll explain how to vitalize your home or office workstation beyond the usual capacities of word processing, games, and spreadsheet applications. And we'll introduce you to basic Internet concepts and applications showing how it's possible to travel electronic highways and reach destinations such as Australia or Switzerland in mere seconds. If you're not already connected to the Internet, we'll show you how you can get access with only a computer and a modem. Once you get *hooked* on the Internet and learn how you can communicate electronically with people all over the world and access information from thousands of sources, you'll understand why the phrase *exponential growth* is mentioned in virtually every article about the Internet. Computers are becoming more powerful and less expensive. More importantly, they are rapidly being connected to allow people to communicate and share information.

You've likely heard of—or even used—CompuServe or Prodigy, the commercial networks and information providers. On the Internet you can travel far beyond the electronic malls of the commercial services and reach many more people, for it is much more powerful. It is not diffuclt to understand the Internet. Indeed, learning to use the Internet has been compared—as have many new skills—with learning to ride a bicycle. You have to make the effort to stay upright on a two-wheeler—or else resign yourself to riding a tricycle. So, too, learning the Internet requires some commitment, but the results are well worthwhile. Until the last few years, the Internet was the sole province of researchers and computerphiles who had neither the interest, the need, nor the time to make a friendly user interface. Fortunately, this is beginning to change, and a concern for user-friendliness is dominating many planning efforts.

Internet access and interfaces vary tremendously, but you don't have to be a computer expert to use the applications or understand the concepts. *The Internet Companion* will serve as your guide, helping you find the path toward information you need and telling you everything you need to know to get started. It also will show you how to get more information, with a thorough bibliography and an appendix of sources and resources full of free online books, hypercard stacks, and guides.

The Internet Companion is full of examples and sample commands to try. In general, computer names and email addresses by themselves appear in italics. New terms are introduced in boldface. Some of the example commands are a mixture of bold and italics; in those cases, you should type anything in bold *exactly* as it appears. The italics represent variable input that only you can supply, such as your email address, or your login name.

Keep in mind that the guidance offered in this book is general by necessity—we can't offer step-by-step directions that will fit every case. Furthermore, the Internet is constantly growing and changing, and new services are being made available on a daily basis. It's exciting, but difficult to document. The resource information included was up-to-date when the book went to press, but it is possible that some of it will have changed by the time you read it. Just remember always to read any instructions that are given when connecting to an online database, and if you have problems, consult your provider's helpdesk or consulting services.

So take a walk on the digital frontier! Get ready for the next installment of the Information Age! Despite the fact that the authors have never met face-to-face and live almost 2000 miles apart, we were able to write this book in less than eight weeks by exchanging ideas and drafts through the Internet. If *we* can do that, just think about what *you* can accomplish! If you have comments about the book, or if you have an interesting tale to tell about how the Internet has changed your life, send an email message to *internet-companion@world.std.com*.

September 1992   Tracy LaQuey, *Austin, Texas*
                         Jeanne C. Ryer, *North Sandwich,*
                                            New Hampshire

Acknowledgments

We thank our husbands, Patrick Parker and Philip Wilcox, and our families for their support and encouragement. Laura Fillmore, our agent and *provocateur*, gave us the necessary motivation to keep going, Tim Evans assisted when deadlines drew near, and Gene Bailey was always available to offer much needed and appreciated advice. The staff at Editorial, Inc. guided us professionally through the editorial and production process. Our editors at Addison-Wesley, Keith Wollman and Elizabeth Rogalin, provided direction and sensitive criticism. We'd like to thank Senator Al Gore for his thoughtful foreword and Michael Nelson of Senator Gore's staff for his assistance. William C. Bard and Tracy LaQuey's colleagues at the University of Texas System Office of Telecommunication Services helped provide her time for the project, and Connie Stout of the Texas Education Network provided encouragement. Guy L. Steele Jr., L. Stuart Vance, and Philip Doty reviewed the manuscript and provided valuable input. The following people also provided valuable advice, information, and assistance: Billy Barron, Kurt Baumann, Duncan Briggs, Steve Campbell, Vinton G. Cerf, Susan Estrada, William Green, Geoff Huston, Ole Jacobsen, Brian Kahin, Brewster Kahle, Peter Kaminski, John C. Klensin, Sarah F. Lester, Jean Armour Polly, Anthony M. Rutkowski, Derek Saunders, and Willem Scholten. We also want to thank all of the people who gave us stories about how they use the Internet.

September 1992 The Authors

Chapter 1

WHY YOU SHOULD KNOW ABOUT THE INTERNET

*T*he *Internet is a loose amalgam* of thousands of computer networks reaching millions of people all over the world. Although its original purpose was to provide researchers with access to expensive hardware resources, the Internet has demonstrated such speed and effectiveness as a communications medium that it has transcended the original mission. Today it's being used by all sorts of people—educators, librarians, hobbyists, and businesspeople—for a variety of purposes, from communicating with each other, to accessing valuable information and resources. To appreciate what the Internet has to offer, imagine discovering a whole system of highways and high-speed connectors that cut hours off your commuting time. Or a library you could use any time of the night or day, with acres of books and resources and unlimited browsing. Or an all-night, nonstop block party with a corner table of kindred souls who welcome your presence at any time. Well, that's the Internet, and this chapter will tell you why you should know about it.

INSTANTANEOUS INFORMATION AND COMMUNICATION

The information age has been ushered in by new and powerful methods of communication. Gutenberg's inven-

1

tion of the printing press took books out of the ecclesiastical libraries and put them into the hands of the people. Then, the telephone system emerged to allow people instantaneous communication with one another. Now the Internet merges both these technologies, bringing people and information together without the middleman (publisher) necessitated by books or the primarily one-to-one synchronous limitations of the telephone system. This is a new dimension—an electronic, virtual world where time and space have almost no meaning. People in geographically distant lands communicate across time zones without ever seeing each other, and information is available 24 hours a day from thousands of places. The implications of this new global communication and information system are staggering.

Instantaneous broadcast of information has been available through television for decades. Much of what we watch, however, is carefully selected and edited according to the discretion and whims of major networks and advertisers. The dawn of a new era in television began in 1991, when much of the world witnessed the bombing of Baghdad as Cable News Network (CNN) provided on-the-ground, uncensored coverage of an historic military event. Throughout the Gulf War, CNN continued to broadcast live from the war zone. Heads of state and generals got their information at the same time as the rest of the world. Consider that this kind of instantaneous, around-the-globe communication was already taking place on the Internet (and other worldwide networks) and, in fact, had been widely used for more than a decade. Although a bit less glamorous—without the video and the heroic flak-jacketed reporters—the Internet hummed with live bulletins during the Gulf War, as it also did during the Tiananmen Square confrontation, the Soviet coup attempt, the civic uprising in Thailand, the riots in Los Angeles, and the civil war in what used to be Yugoslavia.

But there is a difference between television and the Internet. In the Gulf War news coverage, we were the watchers, dependent on a few men and women with cameras and a company with the technology to bring those images home to us. On the Internet, *we* are the reporters, the viewers, and the production team, as well as people just using the networks to talk to colleagues and customers and to get our jobs done. The phrase "democratization of information" often comes up in discussions about the Internet, which is, indeed, a truly democratic forum. The network doesn't care if you're president of a Fortune 500 company or a warehouse clerk, a potato farmer, or a molecular biologist. Your communications are handled the same way, and it's the worth and wit of what you have to say that determines who's willing to listen—not your title. In most cases, you're free to say what you want, when you want. The Internet is an open and sharing environment that's remarkably free of censorship, a tribute to its roots in the academic and research communities.

FROM WHENCE IT CAME

The Internet was not, of course, born full-blown in its present worldwide form of thousands of networks and connections. It had a humble—but exciting—beginning as *one* network called the ARPANET, the "Mother of the Internet." The ARPANET began as a U.S. government experiment in packet-switched networking back in 1969. ARPA, the Department of Defense (DOD) Advanced Research Projects Agency (which later became DARPA, the Defense Advanced Research Projects Agency), initially linked researchers with remote computer centers, allowing them to share hardware and software resources such as computer disk space, databases, and computers. Other experimental networks using packet radio and satellite were connected with the ARPANET by using an internetwork technology sponsored by DARPA. The original ARPANET itself split into two networks in the early 1980s, the ARPANET and Milnet (an unclassified military network), but connections made between the networks allowed communication to continue. At first this interconnection of experimental and production networks was called the DARPA

A Coup on the Internet

During the coup attempt that spelled the end of the Soviet Union in August of 1991, a small email company with an Internet connection found itself one of the few unrestricted communications media left. The government appeared to be jamming the radio stations and tried to ban all newspapers. Soviet TV programmed old movies and opera. Attempts were made to cut off the Western media.

The only email carrier in the Soviet Union (that charged in rubles) to offer domestic service and international connections at that time, Relcom (RELiable COMmunications) was a small network by Western standards, supplying just under 400 organizations email access mainly by dialups over the telephone lines. Subscribers typically connected to Relcom using personal computers and their own modems, which gave them Internet email access in an indirect way.

With Gorbachev and glasnost under arrest, Relcom's team of entrepreneurs and technicians keyboarded and posted releases in both English and Russian from the banned newspapers and news agencies, Boris Yeltsin's defiant decrees (hand-delivered from his headquarters), and man-in-the-street reports from their subscribers. Major Western news sources such as AP and CNN began using it.

(Continued)

Internet, but later the name was shortened to just "the Internet."

Access to the ARPANET in the early years was limited to the military, defense contractors, and universities doing defense research. Cooperative, decentralized networks such as UUCP, a worldwide UNIX communications network, and USENET (User's Network) came into being in the late 1970s, initially serving the university community and later on

At the same time, Relcom's Internet connection became a key source of news on the coup for the Soviet people. Relcom staffers asked for and got massive amounts of email from outside the country, including news from CNN. As one of its subscribers wrote later, "When the dark night fell upon Moscow, Relcom was one source of light for us. Thanks to these brave people we could get information and hope."

There were days of intense danger at first. Relcom's computer was only a mile from KGB headquarters. "Don't worry, we're OK," wrote one of Relcom's staffers, "though angry and frightened. Moscow is full of tanks and military machines—I hate them. . . . Now we transmit information enough to put us in prison for the rest of our life."

What got Relcom through to the outside world? Sheer courage was part of it. There was also what one of Relcom's hackers called "a subliminal professional kernel"; the staff soon set up a diffused network with reserve nodes and secret locations, and the authorities never caught up with them. And beyond that, of course, there was the great, big illuminating cloud of the Internet itself.

Derived from a paper by Larry Press, Professor of Computer Information Systems at California State University, Dominguez Hills. Published in full in the proceedings of iNet '92 in Kobe, Japan (June 15–18, 1992).

commercial organizations. In the early 1980s more coordinated networks, such as the Computer Science Network (CSNET) and BITNET, began providing nationwide networking to the academic and research communities. These networks were not part of the Internet, but later special connections were made to allow the exchange of information between the various communities.

The next big moment in Internet history was the birth

of the National Science Foundation Network (NSFNET) in 1986, which linked researchers across the country with five supercomputer centers. Soon expanded to connect the mid-level and statewide academic networks that connected universities and research consortiums, the NSFNET began to replace the ARPANET for research networking. The ARPANET was honorably discharged (and dismantled) in March 1990. CSNET soon found that many of its early members (computer science departments) were connected via the NSFNET, so it too ceased to exist in 1991.

BIGGER, FASTER, BETTER

Around the time NSFNET was built, the Internet began growing by leaps and bounds, showing exponential gains in number of networks, human participants, and computers. Similar international networks sprang up rapidly all over the world and connected to the U.S. nets. For example, there are now Internet connections to networks in Australia, the Nordic countries, the U.K., France, Germany, Canada, and Japan. Networks in South America are beginning to connect to the Internet, but as yet there isn't a significant Internet presence in Africa.

Internet fever continues, growing almost unabated, as more and more organizations scramble to get their networks connected. The current Internet (that's today, as we write this book) consists of more than 8000 networks literally spanning the globe. It extends to 45 countries on all seven continents. (Yes, there's even an Internet connection to Antarctica!) One estimate, cited by Senator Al Gore in a recent issue of *Scientific American*, has the amount of traffic on the Internet growing by 10 per cent each *month*. It's been estimated that between 5 and 10 million people use the Internet itself and that upwards of 25 million people can exchange online messages between the Internet and all of the other interconnecting networks. (See Chapter 2 for an explanation of these connections.)

Overall, the Internet is the fastest global network

EXPONENTIAL GROWTH IN NUMBER OF COMPUTERS

In 1981, 213 computers were registered on the Internet; by 1989 there were 80,000. In October 1990, there were 313,000; only three months later, in January 1991, there were 376,000. And in January 1992, there were 727,000 Internet registered computers. If this trend continues, there should be almost 1.5 million by the time this book is in your hands. And these figures are considered to be conservative estimates!

Source: Mark Lottor, "Internet Growth (1981–1991); RFC 1296," *Network Working Group Request for Comments*, Network Information Systems Center, SRI International, Menlo Park, Calif., January 1992.

around. Speed is often referred to as **throughput**—how fast information can be propelled through the network. As we'll see in the next chapter, the Internet isn't just *one* speed, because it can accommodate both slow networks and the latest technology. The NSFNET in the United States currently has the fastest overall speeds, capable of transmitting 45 megabits per second (about 5,000 typescript pages). Gigabit-per-second network speeds currently being tested will allow even more advanced applications and services, such as complex weather prediction models produced by supercomputers and transmitted to weather centers.

While exponential growth and high speed certainly contribute to the Internet's reputation as a notable network, another reason is its success in achieving **interoperability**. Interoperability is the capacity of many diverse systems to work together to enable communication. It can occur only if the computers and the network hardware adhere to certain standards.

Although you may not think about it often, standards play a big part in your everyday life. Camera film always fits in your camera, and looseleaf paper bought at the drugstore fits in your binder. Libraries catalog books according to a standard system, so that once you learn it, you can walk

A Marriage Made on the Internet

Rodrigo and I met in Guatemala about 7 years ago, when we were both studying computer science, and became casual friends, nothing more. In 1990 we both left Guatemala to pursue grad studies at different universities in the U.S.

In January of 1991 we exchanged email addresses and started corresponding. We discussed every-thing from our studies, to the latest news on the *soc.culture.latin-america* newsgroup.

By mid-February he was already ending his mes-sages by sending me "a hug." Internet email was what really allowed us to share our interests, coursework, and ideas and to get to know each other in the same way that lovers used to do through letter writing.

Since he insinuated that he would like to see me, I packed my bags and, to his surprise, flew to New York that summer . . . and everything went very well!

From then on our email usage increased, plus we started "talking" interactively on the Internet for hours at a time, every other night. Rodrigo finished his coursework and went back to Guatemala. Our country does not have reliable postal services, and with the extremely high phone rates, it would have been very difficult for us to stay in touch without email. The Central American region does not yet have Internet nodes, but there is one UUCP node in Costa Rica, *huracan*, of which Rodrigo has become an avid user.

So for the last six months we have communicated through that node. Since we're getting married in August, now we're talking wedding arrangements. And yes, we are sending out an electronic invitation to all our "electronic acquaintances."

Source: Grete Pasch

into any library and find the books you need. Things that don't conform to standards, on the contrary, can make your life miserable. Standards are just as important in the computer and networking world. Without standards, only similar computers could talk to each other, creating an electronic Tower of Babel. The standards, or **protocols**, that the Internet uses are considered "open," meaning that they're publicly available, and they enable disparate computers from many vendors to talk to each other. Chapter 2 will explain this concept further, as well as how the protocols and the networks fit together to make the Internet work.

THE NETWORK COMMUNITY

The Internet community is expanding not only in numbers but in breadth of application. The Internet has always been, and will always be, a key part of the research and development community, but the increase in access and the network's potential for becoming the basis for worldwide communication between people in all walks of life cannot be ignored by the rest of us. A network that was once the sole province of researchers—and, well, geeks—is now home to third-graders, political activists, farmers, and librarians, as well.

Journalists use the Internet to cover topics from the computer business to current events, and some even conduct interviews electronically. Medical researchers share information on diseases such as AIDS. Doctors transmit x-ray or CAT-scan images to medical centers for further analysis. There are bulletin boards for artists and online archives for agriculture. Elementary and high school students travel the Internet in geography and language arts lessons, learning about other cultures. Librarians love the Internet for its advanced document searching tools and the almost instant access to the catalogs and archives of major libraries all over the world. Business people contact clients and accept orders over the network, and many are beginning to print email addresses on their business cards.

In short, the Internet gives you access to more people and more information faster than you can imagine, including online catalogs from most major U.S. academic and research libraries and from more and more foreign libraries. All told there are at least 500 libraries' catalogs, and more are being added almost daily.

In addition to research resources, the Internet is also beginning to resemble the commercial information/database providers like CompuServe and Prodigy in offering up-to-date weather, travel information, restaurant reviews, recipe archives, and access to UPI newsfeeds and valuable commercial legal and business information databases for a fee. The free resources still outnumber the commercial ones, however, which makes exploring the Internet fun. We'll tell you how to tap into this worldwide community of people and information in Chapters 3 and 4.

The Politicians

The potential political impact of the Internet hasn't gone unnoticed on either the national or global political scene. The Tiananmen Square bloodshed, the Yugoslavian civil war, the fall of communism, the Los Angeles riots—all were described by people who witnessed the action and transmitted live reports across the Internet. The Internet has, indeed, played a large part in disseminating information while events were unfolding.

Political candidates are starting to realize the benefits of instantaneous broadcast of information to large groups of people. In this presidential election year, most of the candidates had email addresses that could be reached from the Internet. The election in general and political platforms in particular were discussed in great detail in certain electronic forums. In the future, electronic town meetings will be the norm.

The Internet, the Environment, and the Law

Operating under the premise that information is like water in a desert, a group of environmental lawyers are using the Internet to provide access to scientific and legal information to environmental action groups in the developing world.

Environmental Law Alliance Worldwide (E-LAW) was formed by public interest lawyers in Peru, Ecuador, Australia, Malaysia, Indonesia, the Philippines, Sri Lanka, and the U.S. E-LAW uses email and conferencing, starting with the EcoNet/PeaceNet system in the U.S., and is distributed throughout the world on the Internet, BITNET, and UUCP. Their success in networking to remote sites and undeveloped regions has been inspiring to other international groups.

Does it work? According to John Bonine, a professor of Law at the University of Oregon, "Ecuadorian public interest lawyers have been fighting to prevent oil drilling in a National Park in the Amazon considered to be the most biologically diverse on the planet. They uncovered information on improper influences in the Ecuadorian judicial system by certain foreign oil companies, drew up a complaint to the U.S. government, and publicized the complaint worldwide on the computer networks." This effort, combined with others, may have persuaded a major North American oil company to drop the project.

E-LAW's position is that speedy access to information, whether scientific studies or other legal actions, helps level the playing field between the people trying to protect fragile resources in remote areas of the world and the big multinational companies who have worldwide access to information and the resources to press their points of view.

From an article by John E. Bonine in *Internet Society News,* vol. 1, no. 1 (Winter 1992), p. 26. Published by the Internet Society in Reston, Va.

SatelLife

Physicians in Africa are practicing medicine and dealing with some of this century's most serious medical challenges in the midst of staggering "information poverty." In the mid-80s, the problem caught the attention of Dr. Bernard Lown, founder of International Physicians for the Prevention of Nuclear War (winner of the Nobel Peace Prize in 1985), who felt the high frontier of space should be used for humanitarian rather than military purposes. He started SatelLife, a non-profit organization committed to promoting health in the developing world by providing improved communication and exchange of information. SatelLife's HealthNet is a computer network linking medical centers in the Southern Hemisphere. Using a microsatellite, HealthNet enables physicians and healthcare workers in remote areas to upload and download information to each other and to medical and research centers in the industrialized countries.

For example, a physician treating an AIDS patient in Zambia, Africa, where the HIV-positive rate ap-

(Continued)

The Activists

Activists were among the first to realize the Internet's potential for cheap, fast, global communication. The Internet is a perfect tool for alerting and assembling large numbers of people electronically. Amnesty International, for example, has been using its Urgent Action Network on PeaceNet to mobilize its members to pressure government officials to release political prisoners. It may come as no surprise that dictators and tyrants don't appreciate their actions being made public through this democratic tool.

PeaceNet is part of the Institute for Global Communi-

proaches 25 percent, could better treat his patient by communicating with physicians and researchers in other African countries as well as with colleagues in other parts of the world. Through HealthNet, he can get a free electronic copy of the *New England Journal of Medicine*, with the latest research results, rather than waiting six months to receive a copy that might cost half his monthly salary. Using the HealthNet system, this physician can query researchers about new developments, such as the possible connection between polio vaccines and AIDS in Africa, or about new drugs developed for AIDS treatment.

Staffed by people in Cambridge, Massachusetts, SatelLife received a major contribution for their first satellite from NEC Corp. SatelLife's second satellite is slated to be launched in 1993. With ground stations in Africa (and soon in Brazil), SatelLife stations connect to the Internet through a gateway in Newfoundland. Ultimately, SatelLife hopes to use the Internet, and electronic communication in general, to create partnerships for better health.

Based on an interview with Charles Clements, M.D., Executive Director of SatelLife.

cations (IGC) network, probably the best-known and most efficiently coordinated computer effort for peace and protection of the environment. Through its connection to the Internet, IGC encourages people to "dial locally, act globally" to collaborate on peace issues. Another IGC network, EcoNet, focuses on the many environmental issues affecting our planet and has forums and information on global warming, destruction of the rain forests, legislation affecting environmental programs, toxic chemicals entering the water supply, and education of the general public on environmental issues.

The Internet explosion has had an interesting environmental side-effect, effectively allowing more and more people to telecommute to their jobs. As pressure to reduce air
pollution from automobiles continues to mount, increasing
access to the Internet for ordinary people will allow more
to work at home and leave cars in the garage. Telecommu-
nicating will also give handicapped users the freedom to
travel electronically and give families more time together at
home.

BECOMING PART OF THE INTERNET

Whether you have a PC or a Cray YMP supercomputer, a
high-speed network or a regular telephone line, you can get
connected to the Internet. There are two basic methods of
access available for individuals: through an organization's
network, or through a computer, modem, and telephone
line. The basic costs are explained below, but Chapter 6
discusses some of the available options in more detail and
also tells you the general steps to take if you wish to connect
your organization's network.

Costs

For many people, the Internet is an all-around good deal.
People who have access to the Internet through an organization, such as a university or a large company, don't have
to worry about how much they use the Internet. Their
communication with people from all over the world and
access to most information resources is not going to show
up itemized on a long-distance bill, because the leased lines
or network links are already paid for. For those users, it's
like having a WATS line with no limit.

Individual users without the benefit of organization
apron string links, in contrast, must get their access from
commercial Internet providers, public access Internet sites,
or a digital rich uncle giving away access through public
accounts. Access for those with a computer and a modem
is usually through a local telephone call to a terminal server

or computer. The costs can vary, but many commercial providers charge a flat rate monthly fee that isn't bad compared with the potential gain of instant worldwide communication. Some providers charge as little as $20/month for unlimited electronic mail. But, just as the telephone system still doesn't quite reach everyone worldwide, Internet access is not always easily available or reasonable. Many people in remote areas or foreign countries must make expensive long-distance calls to send and receive electronic mail or to access resources. Often isolated and desiring human contact and access to information, they find the extra cost worth it—*if* they can afford it.

The U.S. National Research and Education Network

Although the Internet is spreading quickly around the world and more and more organizations are connecting to it, not all U.S. academic and research institutions are connected. Recognizing the importance of having the United States maintain technological superiority, Senator Al Gore sponsored a bill, "High-Performance Computing Act of 1991," which was signed into law in December 1991. This authorizing legislation promotes technical leadership by providing all researchers with access to powerful supercomputer resources and valuable information resources. The bill also calls for coordinating and combining several federal agencies' individual networking efforts into one high-capacity, high-speed network that will connect all academic and research institutions and federal agencies. Known as the National Research and Education Network (NREN), this network will, in essence, be the successor to the research and education portion of the Internet in the United States.

"High-speed" in this bill means gigabit-per-second speeds. For example, an entire encyclopedia could be transferred in less than three seconds. This encyclopedia metric is often used to describe how fast the network will be, but it's important to realize that although some advanced applications, such as videoconferencing, will require high speeds, this capacity will be used more to handle the increasing number of people who will be using the network. You can compare this additional capacity to a 10-lane highway: the number of lanes does not enable you to drive 10 times faster; it just allows more cars to travel at the same time.

The NREN will use this added capacity to link researchers with expensive hardware resources such as supercomputers. Access to valuable information databases and online libraries will benefit the "E" in the NREN, the education community, hooking up all of the 2-year and 4-year colleges and universities. And, in addition to all the fancy applications, visualization, and multimedia services that will no doubt appear, remote learning applications, more user-friendly tools, and directories of people and resources are also planned. While all of this should be in place sometime in the mid-1990s, the NREN actually exists now. The NSFNET, the nationwide network connecting the majority of academic and research institutions in the United States, is now referred to as the "Interim NREN." The whole idea is to use existing resources, building on top of the current infrastructure, instead of "reinventing the wheel."

It is imperative that this technology, now readily available to many scientists and researchers, be extended to practical applications in K–12 education, libraries, the health care industry, and manufacturing and be further extended to the home. The NREN will provide the basis for a national public network that will connect grade schools and libraries, hospitals and factories. Already there are a growing number of K–12 schools and districts being connected. The Texas Education Network (TENET), a statewide K–12 education network with a connection to the Internet, currently links over 15,000 educators in Texas. These teachers and administrators are using the network to communicate with other educators all over the world and to access educational resources such as an online encyclopedia, the Educational Resources Information Center Documents Da-

---

The Internet and the Classroom

Patsy Lanclos, a TENET Trainer, is an enthusiastic supporter of the Internet and how it is being used in K–12 classrooms. When asked what she thought of the Internet, she had this to say:

"You know, I think one of the greatest things I have seen regarding TENET and the Internet is the enthusiasm it has put back into teachers. Teachers who were tired and worn have suddenly been retread and are ready to roll! They are out there creating new and innovative lessons incorporating telecommunications of all kinds. They are taking risks. They are asking for the unthinkable—telephone lines in the classrooms and computers! They want to belong. It has created a wonderful network of support. You really aren't out there alone!

"One of the classes became acclimatized to TENET when they wanted to know things in a hurry. Instead of waiting to hear it on the news, read the paper, or listen to the radio, the comments were, 'Let's access the UPI news and find out!' From the Brenham explosion to the California quakes, the news was there instantly."

---

tabase (ERIC), lesson plans, study guides, current events (including daily guides such as *CNN Newsroom* and *Stardate*), and UPI news. It's interesting to note that the growth of this network paralleled the growth of the Internet. The Texas Education Agency predicted there would be, at most, 3,000 participants at the end of the first year of operation; there were 13,000. Texas is not the only state that has initiated K–12 networking projects. Virginia, for example, has a similar network, called the Virginia Public Education Network (VA.PEN).

The Internet and Business Success

According to Alvin Toffler, the well-known futurist, the economic well-being of the United States depends on the continuing development of the networks. "Because so much of business now depends on getting and sending information, companies around the world have been rushing to link their employees through electronic networks. These networks form the key infrastructure of the 21st century, as critical to business success and national economic development as the railroads were in Morse's era."

Source: Alvin Toffler, *Power Shift* (New York: Bantam Books, 1990), p. 102.

The International Commercial Network

The NREN is often compared to the national highway system, as a sort of electronic information freeway built, operated, and funded by the U.S. government. As you'll see in Chapter 2, there are some acceptable use restrictions prohibiting information of a commercial nature on federally sponsored networks, and it's not clear yet how these rules will apply to the future NREN. However, commercial Internet providers are appearing, building their own international networks and offering access to the general public and businesses around the world.

Business people are beginning to realize the importance of being well-connected in order to be more competitive in the global marketplace. New players, such as the new coordinated European market and the former Eastern bloc countries, are broadening the playing field. In order to compete, businesses need the advantages of instant communication and access to valuable information. More and more commercial information providers and networks, such as Dialog and CompuServe, are establishing connections to the Internet, taking advantage of its worldwide reach and allowing their customers more communication options. Recent statistics confirm that commercial organizations are flocking to connect to the Internet in greater numbers than ever. This movement started in late 1990, when the requirement for federal sponsorship of access to the Internet was dropped. The trend shows that many others will be connecting.

THE FUTURE

It's hard to know what will happen in the future. Internet experts don't have a great track record when it comes to predicting how people are actually going to *use* it for their everyday needs. The developers of the early ARPANET envisioned it being used to bring expensive hardware resources closer to researchers. What they didn't expect was that electronic mail would become so heavily used by researchers at geographically distant sites wanting to talk and collaborate with each other. Although the NSFNET was built to connect supercomputers, it is now used more for collaboration and access to information.

As the Internet connects more people and starts to yield more applications, it will be used for more than just electronic mail and transferring files. Internet engineering groups have played with connecting vending machines and household appliances such as toasters and stereos to the Internet, allowing them to be operated remotely. Several recent experiments allowed network engineering meetings in San Diego and Boston to be "virtually attended" by researchers in Australia and Europe and other parts of the United States by transmitting audio and video images of the conference. No doubt, other virtual reality applications incorporating multimedia—sound and graphics—will appear soon.

The future of the Internet, while hard to foretell, will be exciting. Many future applications will make the Internet "transparent" to people who are using it. That is to say, the network and computer will be integrated in the home and office, performing important, vital functions without making you aware of the nitty-gritty details. Already there are interesting applications appearing that are making the Internet easy to use by simply hiding the network details. You don't actually have to know where information is or where resources are located; the applications figure that out for you.

At this point, you're probably less concerned about the future *of* the Internet than about your own immediate future *on* the Internet. So stay with us as we explain a bit about how it works and some concepts you need to know before we take you to this electronic world. Onward to Chapter 2, for the "lowdown" on the Internet.

Chapter 2

INTERNET: THE LOWDOWN

*A*sk an *Internet wizard* what this network is all about, and you'll probably get a long and sawdusty discourse studded with acronyms and techspeak. It's friendly if you approach it right, but potentially huge and terrifying, especially to people who don't know its special ways. In this chapter we'll try to explain some of the basic principles that underlie the Internet. Let's begin with the most important principle of all: You don't have to *fully* understand how the Internet works to use it. Plenty of blissfully unaware Internet users are pounding away at keyboards and communicating merrily, with absolutely no knowledge of how the Internet fits together. But although ignorance may be bliss, the more you know, the more doors are open to you. So here goes.

A NETWORK OF NETWORKS

The Internet is a worldwide web of interconnected university, business, military, and science networks. Why do we say a "web"? Isn't the Internet just one network? Not at all! It is a *network* of networks. The Internet is made up of little Local Area Networks (LANs), city-wide Metropolitan Area Networks (MANs), and huge Wide Area Networks (WANs) connecting computers for organizations all over the world. These networks are hooked together with everything from regular dialup phone lines to high-speed dedicated leased lines, satellites, microwave links, and fiber optic links. And the fact that they're "on" the Internet means that all these networks are interconnected. This network web extends all over the United States and out to the rest of the world, but trying to describe all of it and how it fits together is a bit like trying to count the stars.

In fact, so many networks are interconnected within the Internet that it's impossible to show an accurate, up-to-date picture. Some network maps show the Internet as a cloud, because it's just too complex to draw in all of the links. To complicate matters, lots of new computers and links are being added every day.

So just think of the Internet as a "cloud of links." The cloud hides all the ugly details—the hardware, the physical links, the acronyms, and the network engineers. Remember that you don't actually need to know all the details to communicate and use resources on the Internet.

HOW COMPUTERS TALK

The computers on a network have to be able to talk to each other. To do that they use **protocols**, which are just rules or agreements on how to communicate. Standards were mentioned in Chapter 1 as an important aspect in computer networking. There are lots of protocol standards out there, such as DECnet, SNA, Novell, and Appletalk, but to actually communicate, two computers have to be using the *same* protocol at the *same* time. TCP/IP, which stands for Transmission Control Protocol/Internet Protocol, is the language of the Internet. You may speak Japanese and I may speak English, but if we both speak French, we can communicate. So any computer that wants to communicate on the Internet must "speak" TCP/IP. Developed by DARPA in the 1970s, TCP/IP was part of an experiment in **internetworking**—that is, connecting different types of networks and computer systems. First used on the ARPANET in 1983, it was also implemented and made available at no cost for computers running the Berkeley Software Distribution

(BSD) of the UNIX operating system. TCP/IP, developed using public funds, is considered an open, nonproprietary protocol, and there are now implementations of it for almost every type of computer on the planet. "Nonproprietary" means that no one company—not IBM, not DEC, not Novell—has a lock on the products needed to connect to the Internet. Any number of companies make the hardware and software necessary for the network connection.

TCP/IP isn't the only protocol suite that is considered "open." Since the early 1980s the International Organization for Standardization (ISO) has been developing the Open Systems Interconnection (OSI) protocols. While many of the OSI protocols and applications are still evolving, a few are actually being used in some networks on the Internet, and more are planned. So even though most of the computers speak TCP/IP, the Internet is officially considered a "multi-protocol" network.

The whole idea of protocols and standards can get complicated, but as an Internet neophyte, all you need to be concerned with are the basic applications that TCP/IP offers.

The Internet Toolbox

Three TCP/IP applications—electronic mail, remote login, and file transfer—are the Internet equivalent of the hammer, screwdriver, and crescent wrench in your toolbox. There are plenty of fancier applications using variations on or combinations of these basic tools, but wherever you roam on the Internet, you should have the Big Three available to you. We'll be covering the three basic Internet services in later chapters, but here's a quick introduction to get you on your way.

Electronic mail, also known as **email** or **messaging**, is the most commonly available and most frequently used service on the Internet. Email lets you write and send a text message to another person or to a whole group of people. For example, a third-grade student in Texas can send an

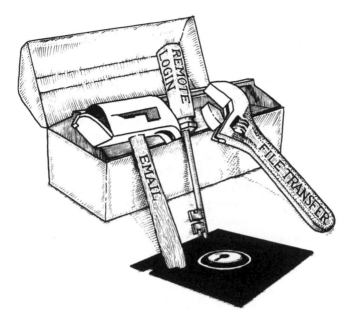

Electronic Mail, File Transfer, and Remote Login are the three basic applications you'll use on the Internet.

email message to a third-grader in Japan to ask how kids spend their free time there. Or a group of teachers can have an email conference on using the Internet in the classroom.

Remote login is an interactive tool that allows you to access the programs and applications available on another computer. Say, for example, that Sven, a student at the University of Oslo, who is heading out to a ski vacation in the Rocky Mountains, wants to check out the weather conditions and snowfall there. An Internet computer at the University of Michigan houses a weather database called the Weather Underground, with temperatures, precipitation, and even earthquake alerts for the entire United States. Sven uses the remote login tool to connect to this computer and interactively query the Weather Underground for the information he needs.

File transfer, the third of the "Big Three" tools, allows

A Very, Very Long Cat

Albert Einstein, when asked to describe radio, replied: "You see, wiretelegraph is a kind of a very, very long cat. You pull his tail in New York and his head is meowing in Los Angeles. Do you understand this? And radio operates exactly the same way: you send signals here, they receive them there. The only difference is that there is no cat." If radio is a very, very long cat, then what is the Internet? A very, very long *tiger*?

Source: UNIX Fortune program.

files to be transferred from one computer to another. A file can be a document, graphics, software, spreadsheets—even sounds! For example, you may be interested in information on Chernobyl from the Library of Congress's "Glasnost" online exhibit of documents from the former Soviet Union. Using file transfer, you can download those articles from the computer they're stored on to your own personal computer, where you can read them, print them out, or clip and incorporate parts of them into a paper you're writing.

How Does TCP/IP Work?

When you're actually using the above-mentioned tools, information of various types is being transferred from one computer to another. TCP/IP breaks this information into chunks called **packets.** Each packet contains a piece of the information or document (several hundred characters, or **bytes**) plus some ID tags, such as the addresses of the sending and receiving computers.

Say you wanted to take apart an old covered bridge in New England and move it lock, stock and barrel to California (people *do* do these things). You would dismantle the sections, label them *very* carefully, and ship them out on three, four, maybe even five different trucks. Some take the northern route and some the southern route, and one just has to go through Texas. The trucks get to California at various times with one arriving a little later than the others, but your careful labels indicate which section goes up first, second, and third.

So each packet, as TCP/IP handles it with its addressing information, can travel just as independently. Because of all the network interconnections, there are often multiple paths to a destination. Just as you might drive a different route to work to save a few minutes here or there, the packets may travel different networks to get to the destination computer. The packets may arrive out of order, but that's okay, because each packet also contains sequence information about where the data it's carrying goes in the document, and the receiving computer can reconstruct the whole enchilada. And that's why the Internet is known as a **packet-switched network.** The switches are computers called **routers**, which are programmed to figure out the best packet routes, just as a travel agent might help you find the best flights with the fewest layovers. Routers are the airport hubs of the Internet which connect the networks and shuttle packets back and forth. The packet is just a chunk of information; it doesn't care (or know) how fast it travels. So it can travel over a "fighter-jet" network, running at Mach-whatever speeds and connecting supercomputers, that interconnects with a "biplane" network operating a lot slower.

The Networks That Make up the Internet

The Internet network connections don't follow any specific model, but there is a hierarchy of sorts. The high-speed central networks are known as **backbones**. The electronic equivalent of an interstate highway system, they accept traffic from and deliver it to the mid-level networks. Mid-level networks, in turn, take traffic from the backbones and distribute it to their own member networks, the neighborhood roads of the networking world. The network links have speed limitations, but speeds are determined by the technology used (not by some "Packet Policeman").

Seamless Worldwide Networking

The bottom line here is that the Internet, which is actually thousands of networks, looks seamless to the user. Also known as the internet-working or internet concept, it hides all the details from you—the packets, the routers, and all those interconnections. Despite legions of different computers and disparate networks, somehow the whole web works, and any computer directly connected to the Internet can talk to all the other computers on the Internet. So you, working on a computer in your office in Iowa or in your spare bedroom in Los Angeles, can communicate with a colleague in South Africa or a friend in Calgary. It's as if you are directly connected by one wire.

WHO RUNS THE INTERNET?

So who controls this web, this cloud, this network of networks? Well, as Christopher Davis, an Internet regular, so concisely put it when asked this question: "Lots of people, and nobody, and the National Science Foundation, kinda, sorta."

Well put. *People* is the operative word here. The Internet seems to be both institutional and anti-institutional at the same time, massive and intimate, organized and chaotic. In a sense the Internet is a cooperative endeavor, with its member networks kicking in money, hardware, maintenance, and technical expertise. The U.S. government has a big influence on the federally funded parts of the Internet. The National Science Foundation (NSF), for example, provides funding to assist academic and research networks in getting started. NSF initiated the NSFNET, the nationwide backbone in the United States that connects these mid-level ~etworks, which in turn connect universities and other organizations. For this reason, NSF sets policy for and operates a chunk of the Internet in the United States, but it does *not* have control over all the mid-level networks it connects.

In addition to the NSFNET there are other federally funded and operated backbones in areas such as the military, space science, and energy research. The Federal Networking Council (FNC) was formed to coordinate these efforts, and it will be working toward combining them into the NREN (see Chapter 1). There are also, of course, many international networks that are overseen by other governments and organizations.

Technical coordination of the Internet is harmonized. For example, the NSFNET backbone is technically managed and operated by Advanced Network & Services, Inc. (ANS), a company established by Merit, Inc., IBM Corporation, and MCI Communications Corporation. Furthermore, the development and improvement of TCP/IP protocols is sanctioned by the Internet Society. Chapter 5 provides more information about that organization.

Of particular interest to business users are the commercial Internet providers that have sprouted up in the United States—companies such as UUNET Communications Services, Performance Systems International (PSI), Advanced Network & Services, Inc., Sprint's Sprintlink, and the California Education and Research Federation Network (CERFnet). UUNET, PSI, Sprint, and CERFnet have interconnected their backbone networks to form the Commercial Internet Exchange, or the CIX (pronounced "kicks"). In addition to connecting organizations' networks, all of these commercial providers offer users with modem-equipped PCs and Macs access to the Internet.

Another interesting undertaking is the Enterprise Integration Network (EINet), being spearheaded by Microelectronics and Computer Technology Corporation (MCC). EINet uses UUNET's nationwide backbone, Alternet, to offer value-added services, an internetwork infrastructure purely in support of business and commercial applications. The appendix contains contact information for all of these providers.

ACCEPTABLE USE

As you can imagine, with all the people and networks and government agencies participating in the Internet, there are bound to be rules, restrictions, and policies for parts of it. Probably the best known and most widely applied is NSFNET's Acceptable Use Policy, which basically states that transmission of "commercial" information or traffic is not allowed across the NSFNET backbone, whereas all information in support of academic and research activities is acceptable.

What is "commercial" traffic? Some examples are purchase orders, invoices, and unsolicited advertising. However, there is a gray area including, for example, announcements of products or software updates. Such information may be acceptable because many times it is considered important and useful to academic and research organizations. Many people also use the Internet to request information about vendors and their products. In this instance, responses—including pricing information—are generally acceptable, because they were solicited by a user.

But restrictions are not universal, especially with the advent of commercial network providers selling Internet access. These providers may or may not have restrictions or acceptable use policies for their own networks. When traffic from their backbones requires passage over the NSFNET, though, things can get a little sticky. Commercial providers usually make their customers aware of acceptable use on other networks.

It sounds somewhat complicated, but you need to remember that the original Internet began as a U.S. government-funded experiment, and no one expected it to become the widespread, heavily used production network it is today. It's going to take a while for commercialization and privatization of these networks to occur. The Internet as a

Living on the Fault Line

One California energy company, Unocal Corp., uses the Internet extensively to give it a competitive edge in the energy exploration business. Earthquakes shake things up in the oil business, so their seismic engineers transfer the latest earthquake data from Caltech to help find potential payoff in their existing geothermal fields. Data from a recent California earthquake was in the hands of the engineers within minutes of release by Caltech.

The company also uses the Internet to get state-of-the-art software for modelling seismic data and technical consulting on the uses of fractals in seismic work. Access to the research community through the Internet keeps the company up to the minute in a very competitive business.

Source: Peter Ho, Unocal Corp.

whole continues to move to support—or at least to allow access to—more and more commercial activity. We may have to deal with some conflicting policies while that process evolves, but at some point in the near Internet future, free enterprise will likely prevail and commercial activity will have a defined place, making the whole issue moot. In the meantime, if you're planning to use the Internet for commercial reasons, make sure that the networks you're using support your kind of activity.

INTERNET CONCEPTS

We'll soon be telling you how to get your hands on the Internet, but before then—as with almost any new adventure in a foreign land—you'll need to acquire a bit of new vocabulary. The basic concepts are simple, and because the network protocols do much of the work, you don't have to become an Internet maven to travel its highways and byways.

Names and Addresses

If you've ever travelled in a country where you couldn't read the street signs or figure out how they numbered the houses, you'll understand the wisdom of learning the Internet's name and address system. Most computers on the Internet can be identified in two ways. Each computer or **host** has a name and a numerical address (both unique), just as most of us can be located by our names or numerically by our phone numbers. It's easier to remember a name than a phone number, and it's the same on the Internet. An Internet computer name is usually several words separated by periods, such as *planet10.yoyodyne.com*. An Internet address, or technically an **IP address,** is four numbers also separated by periods—for example, 161.44.128.70.

When you're saying these names and addresses out loud, to look like you belong you should substitute *dots* for the "periods." This is known as **dotspeak**, and there's a whole lot of it in the Internet. In the examples above, you would say "planet10 dot yoyodyne dot com" and "161 dot 44 dot 128 dot 70."

The idea is for people to use the computers' names when accessing resources and to let the computers and routers work with the IP addresses. Each Internet-connected organization keeps a database of the names and addresses of all the computers connected to its own networks. Because there are so many computers on the Internet and no real central authority, name assignment is best left to the local networks. Imagine if everyone had to get their new phone numbers from Washington, D.C.! The Defense Data Network (DDN) Network Information Center (NIC), which is operated by Government Systems, Inc., in Chantilly, Virginia, does provide a central registering authority in the United States for organizations' second-level domain names and network numbers. Each organization then assumes responsibility for assigning names and numbers to its computers.

So how's it work? When you want to access a public domain software archive on the *wuarchive.wustl.edu* computer, a database at Washington University in St. Louis (the *wustl.edu* domain) is consulted to find out the IP address of that computer. The address (not the name) is passed on to the routers so that they can make the connection. This is done automatically and transparently to you.

Why, then, do you need to know about IP addresses, when the system was designed so that you shouldn't ever need to concern yourself with them? The answer, as you may suspect, is that things don't always work perfectly, and there may come a time when you will need to know an IP address to access a resource. For this reason, many resources are listed with the computer's name and its IP address. The recommended practice is always to use the computer name, since IP numbers—like telephone numbers—can change, while names tend to stay the same (see Chapter 5 for more information on finding IP addresses).

Domain Name System

There's actually a method to these names and addresses: a naming system known as the Domain Name System, or DNS. The DNS is also the worldwide system of distributed databases of names and addresses. These databases provide the "translation" from names to numbers and vice versa, a sort of international *Who's Who* of computers.

DNS names are constructed in a hierarchical naming fashion, which you can think of as a worldwide organization chart. At the top of this chart are top-level specifications, like EDU (educational), COM (commercial), GOV (government), MIL (military), ORG (organizations), NET (networks), and also 2-letter country codes (like US for the United States and CH for Switzerland).

ARMY.MIL MIT.EDU Disney.**COM** Sprintlink.**NET** SwissAir.**CH** Piranha.**BR**
NAVY.**MIL** UTEXAS.EDU Vanhere.**COM** THE.**NET** Fromageries.**CH** Lumber.**BR**

Computer names on the Internet are organized according to the Domain Name System.

An organization can register for a **domain name**, selecting one of the top-level specifications mentioned above that describes it best and then preceding it with a recognizable version of its name. So, for example, the Yoyodyne Software Systems company will have a domain name like *yoyodyne.com*. From there, it can divide itself into subdomains, extending the organization chart to department levels, or it can just give all of its computers names in the *yoyodyne.com* domain.

Once you understand how this naming system works you can remember names more easily, and you can also tell things about a computer, such as to what organization it belongs. The names do not, however, always indicate geographical location. For example, *planet10.yoyodyne.com* may be the main computer at the home office in Grovers Mill,

New Jersey, *mars.yoyodyne.com* may be at the Hong Kong
branch, while *venus.yoyodyne.com* might be located at the
Santa Cruz division.

Many U.S. organizations and companies use the 3-
letter designations mentioned above (for example, EDU,
COM, and ORG). However, most countries have stipulated
that organizations use their 2-letter country codes for top-
level domains. For example, an actual computer name,
quake.think.com, refers to a commercial (COM) enterprise:
The computer's name is *quake* and it belongs to Thinking
Machines Corporation (*think*), a supercomputer manufac-
turer. Another example is *fujitsu.co.jp*, a computer at the
Fujitsu Company in Japan. (*jp* is the 2-letter country code
for Japan.)

Now you probably have a few questions. After learning
about the DNS, every new Internet user first wants to get a
list of all the computers on the Internet. After all, you have
a telephone directory of all the people in your home area.
But there is no exact, up-to-date Internet name and address
list available in hard copy or online anywhere.

In the early days of the ARPANET, a list was maintained
by the DDN's Network Information Center, but the Internet
grew too rapidly to keep up with all the additions and
changes. The distributed domain name system has replaced
this centrally managed list and has allowed the Internet to
grow gracefully.

Internet Resources

While a list of computer names would not be very helpful,
a list of online resources is. **Resources** on the Internet are
all of the useful things that you can access: hardware like
supercomputers, graphics labs, computer centers, or print-
ers. Or online information like the wealth of databases,
documents, software, archives, pictures, and sounds. Resources can also be people. If you can talk to a group of
people to figure out the answer to a question or problem,
they are a resource; so are mailing lists and conferencing

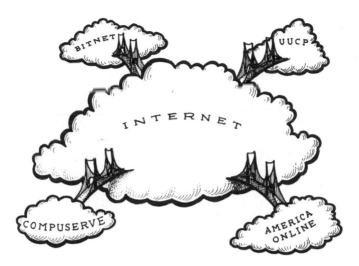

Email gateways allow Internet users to send electronic mail to people on other networks.

systems. An online forum on school networking or a work-group on molecular biology are both Internet resources. Your understanding of the astonishing array of Internet resources, and how to get at them, will grow as you learn your way around the Internet.

Internet or Outernet?

To better understand what the Internet is, you also need to understand what the Internet is *not* and what networks are *not on* the Internet. There are a number of worldwide networks that use protocols other than TCP/IP and provide their own sets of services. Some don't allow remote login, while some employ different file transfer methods; many have a special connection to the Internet. These connections are not, however, the seamless web we were talking about earlier, where the participating networks interoperate to allow the same services. Instead, these are connections of convenience, which—like marriages of the same sort—have their purposes but not a lot of other interaction.

We refer to networks on the outside as **outernets**, but

"Enough of White Man's ASCII"

Dave Hughes, who is kind of an Internet evangel-ist, took to the foothills of the Rocky Mountains to work with a group of Native American teenagers at the American Indian Science and Engineering Society's summer school in physics. According to Dave, the kids, who were from the Navajo, Zuni, Crow, Tohono, Sioux, and Picurus Pueblo tribes, "showed polite, quiet interest as I explained the technology and made a local call to the Internet (Colorado Supernet). They laughed a bit, read, and responded to email sent especially to them by Dr. George Johnston, physicist at MIT, whom I asked to directly 'welcome' them to the world of mathematics and physics by telecom.

"Then I said, 'enough of white man's ASCII' and started calling up the Indian art, the Crow Dance poetry, the new pieces by Lorri Ann Two Bulls, via modem, at 2400 baud. They *really* got excited! Putting questions to me, walking up to look closer at the full-color VGA monitor, their dark eyes laughing,

(Continued)

understanding the distinction between outernets and the Internet can be difficult. Because of the differing govern-ments and languages involved in the Internet and the outernets, there's only one basic service—electronic mail—that currently can move between them. Electronic mail moves from the Internet to the outernets through **email gateways**, the connecting points that translate the different email protocols of each network. More and more of the outernets are setting up email gateways to the Internet. This worldwide system of networks and gateways has been called the **Matrix.** Some network cartographers apply this

smiles, and half of them standing up for the rest of the hour-long session. When it was over, a crowd around the machine, picking up copies of the *Online Access Magazine* and *Boardwatch Magazine* I brought, and more questions. And from their obvious tribal knowledge, they were saying 'That's Crow, that's Sioux!' from the colors and symbols in the various pieces of art.

"A heart-warming session with 40 Indian kids who seemed to get a glimpse of a future even they could participate in. And if I am right, by reaching these youth, starting with their own 'images of their inner selves' as Indians produced by such technologies, they may be better able to move on into the world of science, math, and the cold regions of technological and white man's society, while still not losing their identity or associations with each other. Perhaps even doing their life's work as professionals, from the reservation, thanks to these little devices."

Source: A posting by Dave Hughes to the Consortium for School Networking Discussion Forum List (COSNDISC@BITNIC) on July 10, 1992.

term to the electronic regions discovered during their virtual journeys all over the world via electronic undergrounds and mazes; it's meant to encompass all the possible email passageways. One snapshot of this fast-moving target as it appeared in 1990 was published as a book called *The Matrix: Computer Networks and Conferencing Systems Worldwide,* a sort of Michelin guide for pioneers on the electronic frontier (see Chapter 3 for details on sending mail between networks).

The Matrix is also sometimes called **the Net** by citizens of all networks. This term is ambiguous because it doesn't refer to any one network, but it works well in referring to the overall worldwide situation. If you hear someone say that he's "on the Net," it probably means that he can be contacted by email.

It's interesting to note that many computers on outernets these days have DNS names, so it may only *look* as though they're connected to the Internet. There's a neat feature in the DNS that allows for **Mail Exchange** (MX) computers. An MX computer is a gateway that's connected to the Internet and that is willing (meaning an arrangement has been made) to transfer email to an outernet computer. Instead of finding an IP address for the outernet computer in the database, the DNS obtains an **MX record** or the name of the Internet computer that will deliver the email to the outernet computer. All of this should be transparent to you, making it easier to send and receive electronic mail between the Internet and outernet networks. Which outernets have email gateways to the Internet? More every day, but some of the well-known international networks are: FidoNet, a cooperative network made up of mostly microcomputers linked via telephone lines; BITNET (Because It's Time Network), an academic and research network; and UUCP, a network of computers that talk to each other over dialup connections using UUCP (Unix-to-Unix Copy Protocol). Commercial networks, including CompuServe, MCImail, Genie, and America Online, have made connections, too.

Network News

Another service available on many of these networks is called **network news**. "News" in the network world refers not to current events from the newswires but to discussions, interest groups, and conferences. There are thousands of different discussion groups on topics ranging from artificial intelligence to recipes, from politics to sex, from ornithology to skydiving—collectively generating the equivalent of some 80 books about the size of this one each day. (That's actually about 35 Megabytes of digital information.) News is transmitted on the USENET network, which has special relationships and connections with some of the networks previously mentioned. For example, USENET news can be transmitted across and between the Internet and UUCP networks, allowing citizens of both cultures to participate. USENET is its own network, however, and no one person or organization controls it. It's a huge cooperative anarchy, with 2.5 million people participating worldwide.

Even though USENET is closely related to the Internet and a lot of its traffic travels over the Internet, USENET is *not* the Internet. Many people who have access to USENET news don't have Internet connections; similarly, Internet connectivity doesn't always provide access to USENET news. Also, note that USENET is a conferencing system and is not considered an email network.

Now that we've cleared up what the Internet is and is not, it's time to get on with learning to use it. Conferencing, email, and interactive online conversations are the most exciting new developments in communications since the advent of the telephone. If you think the FAX machine is great, wait until you try the Internet! With just your fingers on the keyboard, you can reach around the world.

Chapter 3

COMMUNICATING WITH PEOPLE

A *network neophyte,* faced with a cryptic computer prompt, may find it hard to picture the Internet as a friendly, peopled place. But every day hundreds of thousands of people are communicating through the Internet—conversing and collaborating, working, playing, and letting off steam. Friendships—even marriages—are made and broken on the Internet. Clubs are formed. Problems are solved. Books like this one are written. Jobs are found. Handicaps and disabilities make no difference. Through email and the other methods of online communication, people have become best friends without ever seeing or talking to each other.

Online communication, perhaps the ultimate in democratic exchange of information, eliminates barriers. You can't make judgments about whom you're "talking" to based on appearance, or even voice. People can be whoever they want to be. Shy people become bold. Children give their views to adults, and the adults "listen." Accounting clerks communicate on the same level as CEOs.

On the Internet, people can communicate asynchronously and in real time. Translation? **Asynchronous** (Greek for "not at the same time") communication means that someone can type in a message and send it off, but the recipient doesn't have to be around to receive it. This type of communication has some real benefits. You can send messages whenever you want to and they reach their destination quickly, and the recipients can read and respond when *they* want to. Answering machines and voice mail are everyday examples of asynchronous communication. **Real-time**, interactive communication, in contrast, means that as someone is "talking" (that is, typing), you see it on your screen as it is typed. We'll be talking about both types of communication in this chapter.

ALL (OR ALMOST ALL) ABOUT ELECTRONIC MAIL

Electronic mail is the most popular application in use on the Internet today. It's a very powerful tool that's simple to use and easy to understand. Using email can give you a real feeling for the energy and reach of "the Net." It's hard to imagine any other form of communication that can be so intimate and yet so wide-reaching, so focused, or so expansive. You can communicate as easily with someone across 12 time zones as with someone in the same building. Your message can be limited to just one person, or it can reach hundreds of kindred souls.

Email is sometimes compared to FAX, but there are some fundamental differences. A FAX is a graphic image that is digitized and sent over regular telephone lines by using modems. Electronic mail on the Internet is text that can be sent over a variety of network links—everything from dialup to fiber optic lines. It usually costs the same to send email to one person as it does to send it to a group of people, while it would probably cost more to send a FAX to those same people, especially if they're a long-distance call away. Both are asynchronous forms of communication, eliminating "telephone tag"—that is, it's not required that the recipient be present to receive either electronic mail or a FAX.

As we said, electronic mail on the Internet is usually text. But it is possible to send other formats, such as graphic images, as long as they're encoded to text before sending and converted back to the original format upon receipt.

email \ee'mayl\ 1. n. Electronic mail automatically passed through computer networks and/or via modems over common-carrier lines. Contrast snail-mail, paper-net, voice net. 2. vt. To send electronic mail.

Oddly enough, the word *emailed* is actually listed in the OED; it means "embossed (with a raised pattern) or arranged in a network." A use from 1480 is given. The word is derived from French *emmailleure*, network.

Source: *The New Hacker's Dictionary,* edited by Eric S. Raymond, with assistance and illustrations by Guy L. Steele Jr. (Cambridge, Mass.: The MIT Press, 1991). Reprinted with permission.

Right now this is not automatically done by most computers on the Internet. Email standards on the Internet are currently moving to support the transfer of nontextual information such as audio, images, and other data; however, this service is not widespread yet.

Sending Email

Email is really fast: It is sent and received in seconds—minutes, at most. Postal mail is often called **snail mail** by way of comparison. Sending email is easy, too. All you need is access to the Internet, an email program, and the email address of the person with whom you wish to communicate.

Access to the Internet.   We've already talked about being directly connected to the Internet or being on an outernet network such as UUCP, BITNET, or a commercial service like America Online. If you have such access, then you're all set.

Email Programs.   You'll need an email program that will run on your own microcomputer or on whatever computer you're using. Most large systems and public access computers offer several email programs (sometimes called email readers or agents). Some commercial Internet service providers will supply programs to load on your PC or Mac. A common characteristic of email programs is that they let you compose and send email, and then read and organize the email you receive. There are too many different email programs to list and explain here. Your choice of a program will depend on how you're accessing the Internet. If you aren't sure what's available, ask your system gurus for assistance.

Email Addresses.   You'll also need an email address for the recipient of your message. An email address, like a postal mail address, contains all the necessary information needed to deliver a message to someone.

Internet email addresses are, in fact, very simple. They consist of a *local part* and a *host part*. The username refers to the mailbox, login name, or userid of the recipient on that computer. For example, if your friend Mike logs into his computer as *Wallace*, then that's his username. The host part of the address should be recognizable to you, a series of words separated by dots, as discussed in Chapter 2. The local part and host part of an email address are separated by an "@" sign:

username@hostname

Let's say that you know Mike's computer name is *60-minutes.cbs.com*. You could send email to him using this address: *wallace@60-minutes.cbs.com*. (This and the following *60 Minutes* examples are fictitious.)

Sending It Off.   Once you have the email program and know the recipient's email address, you're set to send a message. Each email program is different, so if you're not familiar with yours, you may have to fumble around a bit or actually read the manual or online documentation. You will need to specify that you want to *send* a message, either by typing **send,** clicking a *send* button, or performing some

Internet email is usually sent to its destination in seconds.

other wonderful computer incantation. The email program will prompt you for information, asking for the recipient's email address, the key piece of information the program needs to send the message to the recipient. It will also ask for the subject of your message—usually a summary, title, or brief description. The subject is optional, but you should get into the practice of including it. A good description makes the person to whom you're sending aware of the nature of your message, whether it's important or whimsical. The program may give you the option of sending a "carbon copy" (cc) message. If there's someone else you think would be interested in the message, here's a chance to include her address. (You can send carbon copies to more than one recipient.) If you have the disk space, it's a good idea to send a copy to yourself so you'll have a record of your outgoing messages. There may come a day when you'll need to know exactly what you said to someone!

After you've answered all the email program prompts, you can compose your message, using your email program's composer, which may or may not be similar to the word processor with which you're familiar. It's important to make your message easy to read and understand, and we'll explain this further in the "Netiquette" section of this chapter.

Anatomy of an Email Message

An email message has two basic parts, the "header" information and the body of the message. These pieces are separated by a blank line. In most cases, you'll be interested only in the body, or the actual text, of the message. The headers contain items such as "Date:", "cc:", "From:", and "Subject." Sometimes there are seemingly arcane lines such as "Received:" and "Message-Id". These normally don't concern you, but they are necessary in email programs and for debugging purposes. Following is a sample message:

```
From andy Wed Jul 29 08:47:18 1992
Received: by 60-minutes.cbs.com id AA05638
        (5.65+/IDA-1.3.5 for wallace); Wed,
        29 Jul 92 08:47:18 -0500
From: Andy Rooney <andy@60-minutes.cbs.com>
Message-Id: <9207290947.AA05638@60-minutes.cbs.com>
Subject: Did You Ever Wonder Why?
To: wallace@60-minutes.cbs.com (Mike Wallace)
Date: Wed, 29 Jul 92 8:47:18 CDT
Cc: andy
X-Mailer: ELM [version 2.3 PL11]

Hey Mike,

Did you ever wonder why it takes the U.S.
Postal Service 3 days to send a letter? Why 3
days? Why not 2? Or 5? Was *3* the number
rolled on the special Post Office dice? And why
is there no delivery on Sundays? I get a paper
on Sunday. Why can't I get my mail?

Get back to me on this.

—Andy
```

Receiving and Keeping Up With the Mail

Receiving email requires less effort than sending it. Incoming messages are stored in your **inbox.** When you fire up your email program, it checks this online "mailbox" to see if there's anything in it, and if there is, it usually displays a one-line summary for each message in there. You can then select which message you want to read.

If you think you can't keep up with the junk mail that flows into your snail-mailbox each day, then just wait until you collect dozens of "keypals" and you're busily exchanging messages every day. Most everyone just *loves* to get email—it will probably give you a tiny thrill to get the message, "You have new mail," when you check your electronic mailbox. But because it's so easy to send and receive email, you may find that you can't keep up with all the messages you receive! You should set up a good routine for sorting your mail, deleting trivial messages and filing the rest by saving them in separate electronic **folders** sorted by people or topics. If you don't keep up with your email efficiently, as your messages proliferate they stack up in the inbox and your email program may slow to a crawl.

Replying to Email

Email programs usually have some kind of "reply" feature to make responding quicker and easier. For your part, this involves typing **reply** or clicking a *reply* button with your mouse. The reply feature takes care of filling in the address and subject fields (using information in the original message's header) and puts you in the email program composer. A very common convention when replying to messages is to include the original message within your reply message, each line prefaced by a ">" character (or just three spaces). (Your email program may automatically do this for you or provide a command that does it.) That way people can distinguish between their original comments and your response. It may not seem important to explicitly reference parts of the original message, but some people receive so many messages a day that they may not remember your conversation without some background material.

The header lines will alert you to reply messages. For example, a "Re:" will preface the original subject line, and there may also be a "In-Reply-to" line. Let's look at a possible response from Mike to Andy.

The Whole (Email) Shooting Match

Members of the USENET's newsgroup on shooting sports organized the first email rifle competition early in 1992, linking three continents—Australia, North America, and Europe—to schedule, stage, and score a match between smallbore rifle clubs from Liverpool University and the Australian Capital Territory. The competitors did the shooting on their home ranges and forwarded the scoring via Internet email to the newsgroup moderator in the United States, who judged the contest and announced the results.

According to Geoff Miller of the Australian team, making email history was "the easy part" of the project; "then we actually had to get the shooters to the range to shoot their cards!" The Liverpool team, following their leader's red car in a blue minibus, made a faulty fielder's choice at a rotary and took off after the wrong red car. The captain, meantime, mistook another blue minivan for his team's and kept it in his rearview mirror all the way to the range. When the team finally got themselves assembled, he discovered he'd left his rifle at home.

In Canberra, lighting problems on the range led to the cancellation of practice shoots and delays in scheduling the competition. The Aussies took the field on the first weekend of the new year. Hampered by high winds and the aftereffects of the holidays, the ACT team lost to Liverpool by a margin of 50 points.

Geoff Miller, undeterred by his team's showing, anticipates email matches developing into "a regular fixture" on the intercontinental smallbore scene, "providing yet another example of the inexorable march of computers into all areas of life."

```
From wallace Wed Jul 29 08:55:13 1992
Received: by 60-minutes.cbs.com id AA05676
       (5.65+/IDA-1.3.5 for andy); Wed,
       29 Jul 92 08:55:13 -0500        Andy
From: Mike Wallace <wallace@60-minutes.cbs.com>
Message-Id: <9207290947.AA05676@60-minutes.cbs.com>
Subject: Re: Did You Ever Wonder Why?
To: andy@60-minutes.cbs.com (Andy Rooney)
Date: Wed, 29 Jul 92 8:55:13 CDT
Cc: safer (Morley Safer), wallace (Mike Wallace)
In-Reply-To: <9207290947.AA05638@60-minutes.cbs.com>;
       from "Mike Wallace" at Jul 29, 92 8:47 am
X-Mailer: ELM [version 2.3 PL11]


Andy,

> Did you ever wonder why it takes the U.S.
> Post Office 3 days to send a letter? Why 3
> days? Why not 2? Or 5? Was 3 the number
> rolled on the special Post Office dice? And
> why is there no delivery on Sundays? I get a
> paper on Sunday. Why can't I get my mail?

Look, I'm tired of answering these questions.
Why can't you just accept life the way it is?

Mike
```

Bounced Email and Other Errors

Sometimes an email message may not actually reach its destination because of an incorrect address or some other error. Just as postal mail may come back to you stamped "Returned to Sender," you may get a **bounced message** back wrapped in an error message that gives you some clues as to what went wrong. Most often the problem is something you've mistyped in the address. One common error message is *User Unknown,* where the message is received by the computer specified in the address but the local part, or username, doesn't match any username or mailbox on the computer. Most often, the cause is a typo or a misspelling, but if you think you typed correctly, then you should contact the person you're trying to reach by other means to find out the correct username.

Another common error is *Host Unknown*, where the host name is wrong. Again, check for typos first. Sometimes parts of the name are missing—for example, perhaps you forgot to include part of the domain name.

Other bounced messages such as *network unreachable*, (the computer) *can't send for several days, connection timed out* or *connection refused*, and *bad file number* usually have something to do with problems on the network or the destination computer. Most of the time these problems are beyond your control, so you should contact your system consultants for assistance.

Most of the time, if you type something wrong or have an incorrect address, you will get a bounced message. Sometimes, however, your email will simply disappear into the elusive **black hole**, the place where lost messages go and where they'll never be heard from again—or at least that's what it feels like. There are several possible causes of this phenomenon. The message may arrive at the intended destination, where an error is detected, but if your own return address is incorrect, then the bounced message can't be sent to you. Or, the message may arrive safe and sound, but your friend never reads it or decides not to respond to it. Usually, trying again, using another addressing method, or contacting your friend by other means to find out if the message was received will help you figure out what went wrong.

Finding Email Addresses

Probably the most frequent burning question from new users is how to find out someone's email address. Unfortunately, there's no comprehensive online directory assistance at this time, as there is for finding out telephone numbers. There are ways, though, to find email addresses, and the more proficient you become in using the Internet, the more tricks you'll be able to use. There's no harm, of course, in just calling someone and asking.

A new trend these days is to include email addresses on business cards, so when trying to reach a business associate, remember that and check there first. Or just guess—a frequently used and often successful method, believe it or not! If you know where someone works, you can guess at the domain name. Many organizations now allow email to be delivered to *person-name@domain-name*, where *person-name* is either the person's last name or the first and last name separated by a dot (as in *lesley.stahl*) where, like the company mailroom, an email "hub" at the *domain-name* may distribute all the email to the correct computers internally. This is not standard, though, so don't count on it working every time.

Online directory service databases are springing up around the Internet. Many organizations have their own online "white pages," named after the white pages in phone books, but they are by no means universal. We've included more information in Chapter 5 which will tell you about some of the various white pages services.

Sending Email to Other Networks

As we mentioned in Chapter 2, electronic mail is the one application that can be sent between the Internet and outernets. Most networks offer an electronic mail service, and many are connecting to the Internet by email gateways. (Remember, email gateways are computers that have connections to both networks and know how to translate the different email languages between those networks.) So, for example, if you have a friend or client who has an account on CompuServe and you're on the Internet, you can send electronic mail to him or her, and vice versa.

Sometimes, sending email between networks is a bit tricky because you might have to specify a little bit more

FROM THE INTERNET TO THE OUTERNETS

Internet to:	*Syntax*
America Online	*user*@**aol.com**
Applelink	*user*@**applelink.apple.com**
ATTMail	*user*@**attmail.com**
BITNET	*user*@*host*.**bitnet** *user*%*host*.**bitnet**@*gateway* May need to explicitly specify an email gateway, such as **cunyvm.cuny.edu.**
CompuServe	*userid*@**compuserve.com** Convert the "," in the CompuServe userid to a "." Example, **12345,678** becomes **12345.678**@**compuserve.com.**
MCIMail	*userid*@**mcimail.com** Eliminate hyphen in userid. Example MCI address: **123-4567** becomes **1234567**@**mcimail.com.**
UUCP	*user*@*host*.**uucp** *user*%*host*.**uucp**@*gateway* *user*@*domain-name* (if UUCP node has a DNS name)

Source: *Inter-Network Mail Guide,* by John J. Chew, and *The User's Direc-tory of Computer Networks,* edited by Tracy L. LaQuey.

In the preceding table, words in **boldface** should be copied literally when constructing an email address. Words in *italics* should be replaced with the appropriate host, username, or gateway name. This table shows the most common syntaxes for sending email from the Internet to another network. If these syntaxes don't work for you, contact your system consultants. Note that some commercial services charge a small fee for incoming and outgo-ing Internet messages. Many, many more networks have connections to the Internet. For more information and references, see the resources listing at the end of this book.

information in the email address, such as the actual name of the email gateway. If you have to do that, your email address might look like this:

```
username%hostname@gateway-hostname
```

Here, the email will be sent to *gateway-hostname*, which will then deliver it to the *username* at the *hostname*. For example,

```
morley%TV60MIN.bitnet@cunyvm.cuny.edu
```

would send the message to *morley* at the *TV60MIN* node, through the *cunyvm.cuny.edu* gateway.

The MX records we mentioned in Chapter 2 may come into play and bail you out. If the outernet computer to which you're sending email has a DNS name, then you can just use that. You don't need to specify a gateway explicitly; the DNS database will figure that out for you.

CONFERENCING: GROUP SPEAK

You can limit your use of email to swapping "letters"—just like your regular snail mail, only faster—but its electronic nature allows another dimension entirely. Imagine a newsletter focused on your interests, where every subscriber is also a writer and the articles and information all flow around in hours or days instead of weeks or months. Imagine being able to send a question to a group and receive responses from 12 different people from all over the world in a matter of hours. Online conferencing can do just that. Some discussions and conferences are more opinion-centered than work-centered, more like a newspaper's editorial page except that the opinions, commentary, and letters are all online and are sent to every member of the list or newsgroup, not just the editor. There are interest groups for everyone, centered on business, academia, research, games, humor, and hobbies—you name it. The possibilities for information sharing, problem solving, and—let's admit it—recreation, are staggering.

Email Lists

Once you start using the Internet, you'll notice people talking about joining **lists** and participating in discussions on various subjects. They're referring to **electronic mailing lists**, which are group discussions or interest groups. Email lists can involve as few as two people or as many as thousands. There are about 2,600 different mailing lists on subjects ranging from cooking to etymology, from music to genealogy. And if there's not a list on a subject you are interested in, then you might be able to create one yourself.

A mailing list is simply a list of email addresses of people interested in a certain subject. Each list has its own distribution address, which looks just like the email addresses described above. All you have to do to get involved in an interest group is to request to be added or "subscribed" to it by sending email to the list administrator, a regular human being. Your email address will be added to the list and you'll start receiving discussion contributions from other list members. You may reply to these messages or send new thought-provoking topics at any time. Any message you send to the email list address will be distributed to every member of that list. You don't *have* to actively participate by sending messages all the time; you can just "listen" to the discussion. Such listeners are often called **lurkers** (with no derogatory connotation).

```
The Bungee Jumpers Email List
List name:     Bungee-Jumpers
Description:   Find out where the best bungee
               jumping is. Discuss new techniques.
               Testimonials from those who have
               done it. Forum for organizing
               group bungee jumps.
List address:  bungee-jumpers@big-bridge.org
List members:  Evel.Knievel@motorcycles.org
               gene.titus@stunts.tv.org
               charley.devany@banzai.edu
               gordon.smith@fiesta.sa.tx.us
               wallace@60-minutes.cbs.com
```

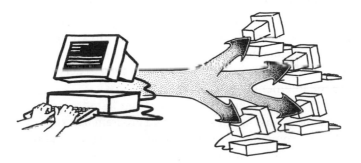

Send one message to many people on an Internet email list.

As we said, to subscribe to an email list on the Internet, generally speaking, you send subscription requests to the list's administrative address, which is separate from the actual list address. In most cases, the administrative address is the same as the list address, but it will have *-request* added to the end of the list name. Let's use our Bungee Jumpers List example above. If this list really existed and you wanted to subscribe to it, you would send email to the administrative address

```
bungee-jumpers-request@big-bridge.org
```

and then state your request. (For example, "I'd like to subscribe to the bungee-jumpers list, please. My email address is," etc.) in the body of the message. The list administrator will add you to the list and you'll start receiving any messages sent from fellow bungee jumpers. (You can also *un*subscribe with a similar request sent to that address.) A common new user mistake is to send subscription requests to the regular list address—a quick way to annoy the other list members, because it adds unnecessary mail to their already burgeoning inboxes. So don't forget about the administrative address.

LISTSERV

A cousin to the Internet email list is the BITNET LISTSERV.

You will hear LISTSERV mentioned a lot because there are hundreds and hundreds of interesting LISTSERV groups. You may want to join one, so it's important to know what they are. Remember that BITNET is an outernet-type network, and the only application that can be sent between it and the Internet is electronic mail.

LISTSERV, which gets its name from "list server," is an automatic discussion list service. It's a program that runs on a BITNET computer (or BITNET node) and handles all the list administrative functions such as subscribing and unsubscribing people to and from interest groups. There isn't such a powerful automatic list maintainer on the Internet yet, where most subscription requests are still processed by an actual person, a maintainer of each list.

A LISTSERV accepts commands requesting different actions, such as subscribing to a list or listing members of a group. On BITNET these commands can be sent to the LISTSERV using an interactive message facility. If you're coming from the Internet, however, you have to send commands within an email message to the LISTSERV address. After the LISTSERV performs the requested functions, it will send you a status report via email so that you will know what happened.

Now, here's the tricky part. The actual BITNET interest group will also have a different email address from that of the LISTSERV. What we mean is that discussion messages are sent to the list address, while commands are sent to the LISTSERV address. Many people get these two confused and end up sending LISTSERV commands to the actual list, whereupon everyone ends up getting a copy of your command message. Let's show an example so that you'll know what we're talking about. Let's say you want to join the World Champion Pro Wrestling discussion group (fabricated for the purposes of this book, but it does have possibilities!). The list address is *PRO-WRESTLING@HHOGAN*. The LISTSERV address is *LISTSERV@HHOGAN*.

Note that BITNET addresses are different from Internet addresses. A BITNET computer name is easy to recognize because it's usually one word (no dots) and sometimes cryptic looking. When you're sending email from the Internet *to* BITNET, you will need to alert your computer to that fact. Usually you can just append *.bitnet* to the end of the BITNET node name, and your system will know how to deal with it. In some cases, however, you may need to specify the actual email gateway, as mentioned above.

Since you want to subscribe to this list, you should send an email message to the LISTSERV address

LISTSERV@HHOGAN.bitnet

because you always send list *commands* to the LISTSERV address, *not* the actual mailing list address. Remember, it's the LISTSERV program that takes care of these administrative functions. Within the body of the message (you don't have to put anything in the subject field), you have to type the following command:

SUBSCRIBE PRO-WRESTLING Ric Flair

(This is assuming your name is Ric Flair. If it isn't, then put your own name in place of his.) As you can see in this example, the *SUBSCRIBE* command is easy:

SUBSCRIBE *List-Name Your-Name*

Your-Name should be your name as you usually write it, *not* your userid or email address. (The LISTSERV gets your email address from the message header, not the body.)

Once you've put this command in the body of the message, you can send it. You should receive a welcome message back saying that you are subscribed and giving you some important information about the list. You'll then get messages about the latest match between Hulk Hogan and the Junk Yard Dog. Now, if you want to participate in the discussion—that is, send messages to this list—then you should send email to the list address, *not* the LISTSERV address. So you would send your contribution to *PRO-WRESTLING@HHOGAN.bitnet*. If you want to unsubscribe, repeat the steps given above, sending email to the

---

Elvis Sighted on Internet

LIVERPOOL NY—But was he wearing a disguise? Elvis has the Internet all shook up with reports that he's been making phantom appearances on the Net! The King has an email account at the Liverpool (N.Y.) Public Library Even the local Liverpool media anxiously await a physical manifestation to confirm whether the presence is the young Elvis or the old Elvis. According to Jean Armour Polly at the library, Elvis does receive mail there, most recently an announcement of a LISTSERV interest group devoted to 78 rpm records. So write Elvis at *elvis@lpl.org* if you've got a burning question about burning love, want to debate the vocal characteristics of the hound dog, or develop a newsgroup on the historical and sartorial legacy of the blue suede shoe. . . .

LISTSERV address, but instead of the *SUBSCRIBE* command you type **SIGNOFF PRO-WRESTLING** and that's it.

There are many other LISTSERV commands besides *SUBSCRIBE* and *SIGNOFF*. If you're interested in learning more, send email to *LISTSERV@BITNIC.bitnet,* with just the command **INFO REFCARD** in the body of the message. You'll receive an email message containing a list of general user commands from the LISTSERV at the BITNET Network Information Center (BITNIC).

List Caveats

If you join an email or LISTSERV list, how much traffic will you receive? That depends. Some lists aren't very active at all, so you might see only a few messages a week. Other lists can become very animated, however, so you'll see dozens of messages a day. Many people get really excited about joining lists, and so they subscribe to a whole lot of them. Then they get more email than they can handle. It's a good idea to keep track of the lists to which you've subscribed. That way, if you go on vacation for an extended period of time and don't want to deal with hundreds (or thousands) of email messages when you return, you can unsubscribe to all of the groups on your list.

The amount of traffic an interest group generates can be reduced considerably if members avoid sending unnecessary messages to the whole list—for example, subscription requests and "I agree," or "Me too," responses. Don't get "reply happy" and feel that you need to respond publicly to every question that someone sends.

Often people use the reply feature in their mail program to offer a contribution to or continue a discussion, or to send a private message to the originator of the message. A word of warning here. You should *always* check to see to *whom* you're replying: Is it the message sender or the entire list? Each email program is different, so you should familiarize yourself with your particular reply feature.

Picture this Maalox moment. You see a message from your best friend on an email list: She has made a contribution to a discussion. You want to reply to her personally and tell her about your bad day and how much you can't stand your boss, so you hit the *reply* button. You use words you shouldn't. You get descriptive in places. You finish the message and away it goes—to every single person on the list, including your boss! As unbelievable as it sounds, it happens all the time. The moral of the story is that you should always double-check to make sure your reply message is going to the right recipients. Either that, or stock up on the antacid pills.

Finding Lists

As we said earlier, there are a lot of lists out there, and they can change quickly. You can download some online "List-of-Lists" and peruse them to find out which groups are for you. Just browsing the A's in one such List-of-Lists, we found interest groups on Addictions, Art, and Animal

Rights. Quite a range. In Chapter 4 we'll tell you how you can use the Internet file transfer application FTP to download (or transfer) publicly available files, such as a "List-of-Lists," to your computer.

LIST OF EMAIL LISTS

A list of Internet and BITNET email lists maintained by SRI International is available via anonymous FTP on host *ftp.nisc.sri.com*, directory *netinfo*, filename *interest-groups*. This file contains descriptions of each list and is about 860K bytes long.

A list of BITNET LISTSERV lists is maintained by BITNIC. Send an email message to *LISTSERV@BITNIC.bitnet*. In the body of the message, type the command **list global**, then send the message. You will receive a rather large document (about 224K bytes) that has the current list of BITNET discussion groups.

See the appendix for more information on lists of email interest groups.

Network News

USENET was mentioned briefly in Chapter 2. It's a worldwide conferencing system, encompassing all sorts of organizations (universities, commercial organizations, government agencies—even home computers) and supporting one service: news. USENET is a real community. People from all walks of life spend hours "together," reading, contributing ("posting"), and responding. Each group has its regulars, its "Norm Petersons." Others come and go. Some "lurk," while others seem to talk incessantly.

USENET is a breeding ground for free expression and thought. People are usually very frank on this network! It's a point of pride that USENET, for the most part, is an open and uncensored environment. As a result, some very explicit and candid discussions ensue, from political argu-

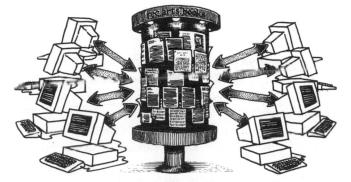

USENET newsgroups are forums for all kinds of interests and topics.

ments, to religious opinions and holy wars, to explicit stories with indecent themes. Be aware of this if you're easily offended and simply avoid the groups that focus on subjects unpalatable to you.

USENET is divided into **newsgroups**. Devoted to a certain topic, each newsgroup is made up of **articles**, which are similar to email list messages. There are over 2,100 different newsgroups on USENET, but not every computer or site gets all of these in its USENET **feed.** Each site can pick which newsgroups it wants to "carry" or let its users participate in. Why wouldn't a site want to provide every single newsgroup? One reason is that the total traffic per day is huge and takes up valuable disk space. Or, the site may be paying long-distance charges to transmit and receive traffic, so it participates only in a small number of groups. Another very common reason is that some of the newsgroups deal with explicit subjects which may or may not be appropriate to carry.

USENET newsgroups are similar to email lists, but there are a few differences. With Internet email lists, every message is sent to each person who has explicitly requested to be a participant. On USENET, every newsgroup article is received and stored on *each* participating USENET *computer*, instead of being sent to each user. Even when you're not participating in a newsgroup, all of its articles are still stored on the computer, so you have easy access to any you want.

USENET Hierarchy and Newsgroup Names.   Newsgroups are organized in a hierarchical structure; their names have dots in them, just like Internet domain names. The top-level (left-most) word in the newsgroup name specifies the newsgroup's category. There are seven major USENET top-level categories, and three alternative categories, as shown below. Knowing what these categories mean can help you figure out what each newsgroup is about.

News Readers.   In order to read or post news, you need to have a news reader program. There are thousands of newsgroups, and you don't want to have to sift through every one of them. A news reader will let *you* select which newsgroups you want to participate in by allowing you to "subscribe" to them (you don't have to send email to an administrator). The reader program will organize the newsgroups, display the articles for you to read, and allow you to post articles. Just as there are many email programs, there are many news readers. Some are user-friendly, while others use terse commands and are difficult to learn.

You'll have to get used to how your news reader works and how it displays newsgroups and articles. Some readers offer a "threaded" functionality that organizes articles within a newsgroup according to discussion threads—a helpful feature if you want to follow a particular discussion within a newsgroup instead of hopping from one debate to another.

If you're not sure about your choices for news readers, check with your system administrator or news provider. If you're on a computer that runs the UNIX operating system, some of the readers that may be available to you include *rn* (for read news) and *vnews* (for visual news). If you're using a PC or Mac and are getting news from a commercial provider, you'll probably have a user-friendly graphical application to use.

MAJOR USENET HIERARCHY CATEGORIES

Category	Explanation
comp	Computer hardware, software, and protocol discussions.
misc	Topics that don't fit anywhere else, such as job hunting, investments, real estate, and fitness.
news	Groups that deal with USENET software, network administration, and informative documents and announcements.
rec	Recreational subjects and hobbies, such as aviation, games, music, and cooking.
sci	Topics in the established sciences, such as space research, logic, mathematics, and physics.
soc	Groups for socializing or discussing social issues or world culture.
talk	Lengthy debates and discussions on various current events and issues—politics, religion, the environment, and so forth.

Alternative Hierarchies

Category	Explanation
alt	Alternative group of discussions: not carried by all USENET sites. Some controversial; others are "lite." Not considered a regular part of the USENET hierarchy. Alt newsgroups generate a lot of traffic.
gnu	Discussions relating to the GNU Project of the Free Software Foundation (FSF). (GNU stands for GNU's, not UNIX.)
biz	Business-related groups.

A Sampling of Newsgroups

rec.arts.books	alt.fan.dave_barry
rec.humor.funny	soc.women
comp.protocols.tcp-ip	news.announce.newsgroups
biz.comp.services	talk.politics.mideast
alt.fishing	misc.education
gnu.announce	sci.military

Springtime in the Ukraine

More and more schools are getting access to the Internet, and seeing its usefulness in teaching geography and social studies, math and science. But the benefits run deeper. A school teacher wrote us about a project where her students communicated with students in the former Soviet Union. "Besides such an obvious social studies application, I was deeply moved by a romantic exchange of notes on springtime in our city and springtime in the Ukraine between a young adolescent girl with cerebral palsy and a young man whose name was Albert." There are no handicapped travellers on the Internet.

Getting Started. Once you're able to access USENET news, the first thing you should do is read all the articles in the *news.announce.newusers* newsgroup. The many useful articles in this group chronicle the history of USENET, explain concepts and common problems, provide a list of frequently asked questions along with the answers, give information on available news readers, explain USENET software and how to become a USENET site, and provide lists of USENET groups. This chapter cannot cover every detail you need to know, but these articles will get you up to speed. This newsgroup (*news.announce.newusers*) is not a discussion group—that is to say, you can't post questions or follow-up articles to it. If you have new-user questions, there is a newsgroup where you can post them: the *news.newusers.questions* group.

Posting Articles. When posting an article in a newsgroup, you're asked for some information. As when you send email, you're asked for a subject. Be descriptive, since there are many people participating and it's polite to give them a good idea of what your posting is about.

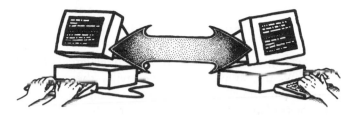

"Talk" or "Internet Relay Chat" gives you interactive communication with other Internet users.

You also need to specify how far and wide you want your article distributed. Many times you'll want to make sure that everyone in the USENET world can read it, but sometimes your article may apply to a local geographic area. For example, if you post an article asking if anyone has any tickets to the Neil Diamond concert on Friday, you probably want to restrict it to your home town of Toronto rather than sending it to Tokyo and everywhere else. It's important that you exercise good judgment not only by specifying geographic areas but also by posting articles only to appropriate newsgroups. For example, it's probably not the best idea to post your resume to *rec.folk-dancing*.

Moderators

The normal operation for most email lists and USENET newsgroups is to let everyone participate, sending or posting whatever they want. As you can imagine, this practice quite often results in what's called a low signal-to-noise ratio— lots of junk submissions that offer little or no quality to the discussion.

As a preventive measure, some email lists and newsgroups are moderated. Instead of being sent straight to the group, messages or articles are submitted to a moderator, who decides whether or not the submission has relevance to the topic at hand. The moderator may submit (or reject) each submission or combine messages and articles to create a digest that gets posted periodically. Moderated lists and newsgroups usually contain a higher proportion of useful

Shared Interests

Teenagers in Texas discovered through email that kids have the same concerns even when they live a world apart. Email exchanges between high-school-age kids in Japan and west Texas covered the common ground of sports, hobbies, pets, and music groups. And a shared dislike for school. "We laughed," Helen Bell, the school librarian at Lincoln Junior High School in El Paso, Texas, said, "when one email told us that 'there are no good teachers in Japan.' "

information, but many people don't like the idea of their postings being evaluated.

INTERACTIVE DISCUSSIONS

So far we've talked about asynchronous communication using email, interest lists, and USENET newsgroups. The Internet also has interactive communication capabilities that allow one-on-one, or many-to-many, discussions. Since communication is happening in real time, you need an interactive connection to the Internet in order to use it. In other words, you can't participate in this type of communication if you're on an outernet network.

Interactive conversations aren't organized into email messages or postings; they are simply displayed on your terminal as they are received. So unless the communications program on your computer allows you to log your conversation, you won't have a permanent record of it.

Can We Talk?

The best-known and most useful interactive communication tool is known as *talk*, which allows you to set up a real-time dialog with another person. Unlike electronic mail or news, both people must be present. Usually a person requests to *talk* to another person by using his email address. For example, if you wanted to chat with your friend Mike, you would use the following command to set up a dialog:

```
talk wallace@60-minutes.cbs.com
```

A message will be displayed on Mike's screen, telling him you wish to talk to him and giving him instructions on how to reach you. If he does indeed want to talk to you, he'll issue the command **talk** *your-email-address*, and a two-way interactive discussion can ensue. The talk program helps you keep "who's typing what" straight by splitting your terminal screen in two. Whatever you type is shown in the top half, while the other person's response is shown in the lower half.

This type of communication is fun, and it can be a very useful tool. It can, however, be somewhat frustrating if you aren't a great typist, for there's a tendency to feel pressure to type as fast as you can— which, of course, introduces all sorts of interesting and creative errors. There's also the "who talks now" problem, for which you have to resort to some radio communication techniques. For example, when you're done typing, you can type **o** for "over," meaning that you'll wait for the other person to type in his response.

The talk capability, unfortunately, is not universally available. There are some implementations on certain types of computers that don't work very well, so you may run into compatibility problems. Also, some system administrators turn this capability off. So you may have to just grin and accept the fact that you can't "talk" with everyone.

Everyone Join In!

The Internet has a many-to-many interactive discussion capability called **Internet Relay Chat**. IRC is considered more of a toy than a tool and is probably used more for recreational purposes than for work. This type of communication is similar to conference calls, where there are several people talking and listening. Michael O'Brien—

a.k.a. Mr. Protocol, the Miss Manners of the Internet—once said, "In general use, it resembles a bank of 900-number party chat lines." If you're a gregarious person who likes to stay up late at night typing in your thoughts and dreams to others, this interactive newsgroup capability may appeal to you. A good place to get started is the IRC Chat Mailing list. Send a subscription request to *irchat-request@cc.tut.fi*.

NETIQUETTE, ETHICS, AND DIGITAL TRICKS OF THE TRADE

It's easy enough to use email and news, but there's an art to communicating effectively online. Here are some general guidelines and some advice, gentle reader, on how to behave.

Listen to Me!

If you want to make sure people "listen" to what you have to say, don't bore and confuse them with rambling messages or postings, which tend to be skipped in favor of shorter messages that concentrate on one subject. If you've got several widely different things to say, it's probably better to organize a bit and send a message on each topic separately. Some people get hundreds of messages a day, so you can't expect them to remember what was said in a previous message. Remember to include background or pertinent material that will help your audience understand the intent of your message.

Some advice on how your message or article should look. There's no hard and fast rule, but a good message size is a screenful or two. Neatness *does* count, and spelling and correct grammar are important. Even though online conversations are informal, sloppy messages that are full of errors really stick out. Take advantage of the asynchronous nature of email and news and spend some time making your message or posting readable.

Limit each line length to 70 characters or less. If you're

creating messages or postings using your word processor, make sure the document is converted to "text with line breaks," meaning that a carriage return is introduced at the end of each line. If you don't do that, your message is going to end up looking funny on the screen and will be very difficult to read.

Try to avoid using acronyms. If you do, here are some that are well known: FYI (for your information), IMHO (in my humble opinion), BTW (by the way), and RTFM (read the friendly manual).

Signing On and Off

There are accepted methods by which to begin and end messages. You almost never begin any message or posting with a salutation such as "Dear Sir." You do, however, initially address the person to whom you're writing ("Andy, I'm looking forward to your show"). Instead of signing off messages and postings with a "Sincerely," or "Love," many people end with their **signature**, which is a sort of digital identifier. Signatures should be short (preferably 4 lines or less) and should include information such as your full name, your organization, and how to reach you. You'll see all sorts of signatures—from very fancy ones, complete with pictures, or cute quotes. Your signature may be included automatically by your news reader or email program, so be careful that it doesn't appear twice. It's good to include a signature in case the addressing information in your message or article header is incorrect or not complete. This might be Andy Rooney's signature:

```
Andy Rooney              1-800-1ROONEY
andy@60-minutes.cbs.com   60 Minutes, CBS
        "Did You Ever Wonder Why?"
```

Beginning Behavior on Newsgroups and Email Lists

You want to be heard, but you don't want to be misunderstood. In addition to making your online communication readable, you need to be considerate of the folks on the other side. Here are a few tips on how to act when you begin participating in newsgroups and email lists on the Internet.

Remember that you're entering a world where there are a lot of experienced folks (including technical gurus and wizards) who have been around a long time. You should treat mailing lists and newsgroups like you do any other club you join for the first time. In other words, don't get on and start blabbing without checking out the territory first. Spend some time just "lurking" to get a feel for the nature of the group and the types of discussions. This background will help you realize what topics have already been discussed in detail and beaten into the ground. It also gives you time to observe the experienced list veterans in action; imitating the experts is definitely recommended. And while you're silently getting up to speed, there's bound to be some other "clueless newbie" who asks the very questions you're itching to send.

New users can't be expected to know everything about discussions that have gone on—sometimes for years. So the "in" thing now is for the "regulars" on mailing lists and newsgroups to compile new-user questions and the answers to them in documents called **Frequently Asked Questions** or **FAQs**. The purpose of these informative articles is to reduce the number of "noise" postings—common questions that everyone has seen a zillion times. Not every group or list has a FAQ, but the ones that do publish them regularly (usually once a month).

See appendix for information on how to obtain some useful FAQs.

Your Invisible Audience

Online conversations are informal. It's much less intimidating to type your thoughts and fire them off to thousands of people than it is to give a presentation, live, in front of the same group. But because you can't see all these people, it's easy to become careless, forgetting to include necessary background information or not thinking about your intended audience. It's also easy to think that because email doesn't use the same conventions we're all used to for paper letters or face-to-face meetings, it is an unrestrained free-for-all. But the net has, in fact, acquired its own conventions and etiquette.

One problem is that electronic conversations are missing body language and voice intonation, crucial components of effective communication. Take these elements away and people are forced to "fill in the blanks" when a typed online message doesn't come across quite right. For some reason, people become much more sensitive when they're on line, and they tend to blow things entirely out of proportion—for example, taking a couple of sentences originally meant to be humorous or sarcastic entirely the wrong way. If that happens, everything can go downhill quickly. Instead of asking for clarification ("You were kidding, weren't you?") or just ignoring it, many people—forgetting that they're dealing with another human being on the other end—decide to defend themselves and tell the originator of the message just exactly what they think of him. This outcome is what's known in the business as a **flame.** If both sides begin insulting each other, it's called a **flame war** (kind of like fighting fire with fire). These digital battles often erupt in "public" and can sometimes be very entertaining to the lurkers.

Friendly Advice

To avoid being involved in a flame war with someone in an electronic public square or a misunderstanding in regular one-on-one communication, follow this advice.

Showing Emotion. First and foremost, you should always be polite and considerate of the folks on the other side. Because you're missing the important visual and aural cues that add nuance to direct conversation, you need to learn how to show emotion online—not an easy task. Probably the most common trick to show emotion is   :-). That's a sideways smiley face (turn your head 90 degrees to the left) used to indicate humor or sarcasm. Since there's no smiley face on the keyboard, you have to "roll your own," using a colon, a hyphen, and a right-end parenthesis. You'll also see variations on the smiley. Sometimes people use a semicolon to indicate winking: ;-). Or a sad face will look like this: :-(.

Upper case is used for shouting, so don't use it unless you want to make a point. For example, if someone wanted to indicate that she was excited or mad, SHE'D SURE AS HECK LET YOU KNOW THAT!!!! Or, she could let you know what she was REALLY thinking by using caps in appropriate places. You can also introduce some online intonation by the use of asterisks in certain places. For example, "This *is* what I meant!" places emphasis on *is*.

Terse Responses.   Terse responses can sound rude. For example, responding to someone's question with only a single sentence, "No, you can't do that!" might make him feel as if he's inconvenienced you, that you can't be bothered to explain *why* he can't do something. If he asked you "live" in person, you'd probably explain. You don't have to be verbose and long-winded, but a few extra sentences will go a long way to insure that you don't hurt someone's feelings.

On the other end, if you receive a short message that leaves you wondering, "What did I do to deserve this?", don't lose too much sleep over it. Perhaps the sender was in a big hurry and didn't have time to explain everything fully.

What may be worse than a terse response is no response at all. Don't expect an immediate response to your email or news queries. People tend to get bogged down in unread and unanswered electronic correspondence. You might get an answer in five minutes—but it also might take five days. Just because you don't hear from someone immediately does not mean that she or he thinks your message was unimportant.

**Always Point a Loaded Mailer or Newsreader at the
Ground.**   Just as you shouldn't drive when you're angry
or upset, you shouldn't send responses to email and news
articles when you're mad at someone. If someone has
"ticked you off" and you're bound and determined to
respond to a message or posting, you should go ahead and
type your response—but don't mail it for at least a day. A
delay may seem frustrating, but chances are that when you
come back later to read your response, you'll be glad you
didn't send it. And you should realize that many times
people will say things just to yank your chain. The thing
these folks want most to see is an emotional, tear-stained
response from you. Don't give them that pleasure!

You should also watch what you say in everyday situ-
ations. A good rule is never to send anything that you
wouldn't mind seeing on the front page of a major newspaper. Online correspondence can be easily archived, refer-
enced at a later date, and sent out to a large number of
people. Avoid saying anything insulting about someone or
disclosing confidential information. Private, sensitive email
messages, or even public flames, could come back to haunt
you someday.

The security and privacy of corporate—and even private—email has caused quite a stir lately, and you've probably got a few concerns about the security of *your* mail. It's
best to resign yourself to the fact that email is not very
secure. Once you transmit an email message, its privacy
depends on the security of the destination system, over
which you basically have no control. Chapter 5 discusses
computer and network security further.

Ethics

As noted, you can't depend on email being secure. About
the only thing you can hope for is that people will behave
themselves and not snoop around in others' accounts,
reading private correspondence. Everyone is under a moral
and ethical obligation to respect other people's property and

wishes. For example, you shouldn't forward private electronic mail to anyone without the permission of the author.
You should also be careful not to violate copyrights by
transmitting another person's work verbatim. There are
other guidelines, but generally you should rely on common
sense and good judgment.

Now that you know how to use Internet to communicate, you will soon be adept at email and conferencing,
LISTSERVs and chat. And no doubt, you're ready to move
on to explore some of those wondrous realms of information resources we've been alluding to. Stay with us. In the
next chapter, we'll look at the information resources on the
Internet, and we'll show you how to use the three basic
Internet tools to tap into the world's online library of
libraries.

Chapter 4

FINDING INFORMATION

Get *ready to switch gears* in this chapter: Instead of communicating with people, we're going digging for information! The Internet has a digital *megaton* of information resources. What's out there? Almost anything you can think of—graphics, software, books, library catalogs, bulletin boards, data, sounds, journals, newsletters, newspapers, magazines, and archives. There are thousands and thousands of independent databases, archives, and online services available via the Internet, making it essentially one big virtual library.

Most information on the Internet is free, although commercial information providers are starting to appear. For example, Dialog Information Services, Inc. now provides online newspaper and professional articles, the *Official Airline Guide*, financial services, and pharmaceutical directories—all accessible to subscribers. The Lexis (for legal research) and Nexis (for business, financial, and regular news) databases from Mead Data Central are also accessible. A company called ClariNet Communications Corporation transmits UPI newsfeeds. And other commercial services are beginning to get their feet wet in the Internet ocean.

Unfortunately, this electronic library is not as well organized as a real library. There isn't just *one* card catalog where you can check to find what's available or where things are located. Part of the problem is that there are just too many computers out there—the electronic universe is truly expanding by the minute. But part of the beauty of the Internet is that it provides access to diverse resources from geographically distant organizations, each with different missions and purposes. And whatever time you can invest in learning your way around will be amply repaid.

CAN YOU GET THERE FROM HERE?

Reading this chapter may tantalize and frustrate those who have only limited access to the Internet. You may be able to reach all of these resources or only some of them. If you're on an outernet network, you're limited to using email servers—where they exist—to retrieve files and access services. Technical, economic, and political barriers are factors that can limit Internet access, but—fortunately for us—nothing in life today changes faster! Your system or provider may add Internet services or connections tomorrow or next month. The restriction of commercial traffic over the NSFNET backbone that we talked about in Chapter 2 may change, too. So experiment and find out what you can and can't get at. If you *really* need access to a particular resource, your system gurus or provider may be able to offer you another path. Once you know what's available, you may find that you need better access. If so, shop around for a connection that offers what you need. Chapter 6 tells you about Internet connection options.

USING ONLINE RESOURCES AND SERVICES

The two basic tools you'll need to access online resources and information are remote login and file transfer. These were briefly mentioned in Chapter 2, but we're going to explore them in more detail in this chapter. Remote login and file transfer both allow you to contact other computers for information and resources, so you can use them only if you are *on* the Internet. Depending on your computer, the tools may operate differently, so read any local documentation or manuals that accompany your software or system. In some cases, you have to type the commands; in others, you may use a straightforward menu system. The examples we use in this chapter will be from a command-level per-spective, showing the commands (in lower case) as you would type them on many computers.

Let Me In!

Despite system differences, you will need to know a few specific pieces of information no matter what your situa-tion. First, you have to know the name of the computer or host that you want to connect to. You'll also need to know the login id and perhaps a password. Most computer systems require that you know the magic word to "be let in" to an account and usually "please" won't work. What's an **ac-count**? It's like your own room in a hotel. You have a key that lets you into your own room (the account), where all your treasured possessions (files) are stored. On a computer, the key is most often a combination of a unique id and a secret password. The id (also known as a username or user-id) lets the computer know who you are, and the password (which only you should know) proves it's really you.

Now, if you live in Amsterdam, it's unlikely that you're going to have an account on a computer in Sydney, unless you have some type of special arrangement with an organi-zation there. But many people do have accounts on remote systems, for various reasons. A real-life example is a profes-sor at a university in the United States who takes a sabbatical to do research in Israel. The professor keeps her accounts open at the U.S. university, and also gets an account on a computer at an Israeli university. If both computers are on the Internet, she can access her files by using file transfer and connect to the services at her home university by using remote login.

Public Services

If you don't have any accounts on other systems, you may be wondering what you can use these tools for. You will have occasions to use them—and more than you may realize at first. Lots (and we do mean *lots*) of organizations are providing services, such as public information and data-bases. To use them, you don't need a personal account on the computers where they reside. (If you do need an account, you're usually given an opportunity to apply for one.) All you need to know is the login id of the service, and that's usually easily available or very well known. Most of these services don't require passwords or, if they do, they either publish them, accept anything as a password, or request that you type in your email address or some other information that lets them track who's using their resources.

A word on the hospitality of people and organizations providing publicly accessible services, file transfer sites, databases, and other resources. Many of these services are made available by volunteers, so act politely and try not to hog resources. Sometimes it's requested that you use a service after working hours, so you should respect that rule, keeping in mind the time zone as well.

Different Environments

When you use remote login or file transfer to access another computer's resources, you are connecting to another environment that may look very different from what you're used to using on your own system. You've probably figured this out by now, but there isn't just "one way" to do things in the Internet world. Different organizations, different computers, and different operating systems all provide different services. Each remote system and service is going to have its particular "look and feel."

The interface—the face that the other computer presents to you—will probably be different. The words may even be in a foreign language. Don't worry, the public interfaces to these systems are pretty robust, so you won't harm anything if you don't know what you're doing and make a few mistakes. Keep in mind that things change on computers, too. Information is added and deleted. Interfaces change. Most of these online services don't come with manuals, so you'll need to read the instructions and use the help screens that are shown when you sign on. It doesn't hurt to make a few notes. A contact name is sometimes listed with the description of the service or on one of the initial login screens; if you have problems, you can email or call. Remember that you're accessing another computer, so your own system gurus may not be able to assist you.

Error Messages

Occasionally when you try to use remote login or file transfer to access resources on other Internet computers, you'll get an error message or just not be able to get to that computer. One or more things may be wrong. First—and most likely—is that you misspelled or mistyped the name of the computer, in which case you'll get a message such as *unknown host*. If that happens, check to make sure you have the right host name. If you're sure you have the right name, then it's possible that this computer simply doesn't exist anymore.

If you know that the computer exists and that you have the correct name and you still get an error message, you can try something else. Remember from Chapter 2 that the Domain Name System (DNS) allows you to use computer names instead of IP addresses. It could be that your computer is having a hard time figuring out what the remote computer's IP address is. If this is the case, and you do know the IP address, you can always try substituting it for the computer name.

If you have the right computer name, and the remote computer doesn't respond after you initiate a remote login or file transfer command, there may be problems with the network or the computer may be "down"—that is, it's not working or available. Just try again later. If the problem persists, contact your network provider or system administrator for more information.

ACCESSING INTERACTIVE SERVICES

Remote login is perhaps the most exciting of the three basic applications. It's a tool that lets you "fly" electronically all over the world, reaching your destination in a fraction of a second. This section will tell you how to connect to other computers and services using remote login.

How It Works

Remote login on the Internet is a lot like using your modem to dial into another computer, but it's usually much faster and you don't actually have to dial a number. The name of the protocol that enables remote login is **Telnet**, which is also the name of the command on many systems to allow you to login to other computers. (Don't confuse "Telnet" with "Telenet," a public data network that was around for a long time.)

When using Telnet to login to a computer, just issue the *telnet* command followed by a space and the name of the computer. (You can also issue the *telnet* command without the computer name, at which point you'll be in command mode. When you see a `telnet>` prompt, you can type commands or **help** for more information.) For example, if you want to connect to NASA's Spacelink, a space-related informational database for K–12 educators and students provided by NASA, just type:

```
telnet spacelink.msfc.nasa.gov
```

When you connect to another system, you are usually greeted by a computerized "Who goes there?" routine. The typical prompt is `Login:` or `Username:`, at which time you type your login id or username followed by the <RETURN> key. If you're accessing a publicly available service such as Spacelink and you don't have a username yet, you can login as **newuser** to apply for an account. Spacelink, in particular, is intended for educational use, but NASA doesn't insist that you be a teacher to get an account. Spacelink is also offered via dialup phone access at (205) 895-0028.

If you already have a username, type it in; you'll then be prompted for your password. When you supply the password, don't worry that it doesn't appear on the screen. It is not shown because your password is supposed to be secret, and you don't want any folks kibbitzing behind you to see what it is.

In some cases when you connect to a resource, you'll have to specify an additional identifier called a **port number**. There can be many services running on a single computer; the port identifier serves to keep them separate. When a port number is required, you usually don't have to type in a username or password. Let's test-drive this command:

```
telnet madlab.sprl.umich.edu 3000
```

Here we had to specify the port number, *3000,* because it identifies the program we want. Resource guides always include the port numbers with the instructions for accessing resources, so if you don't see one, don't worry about it. In this case, we're connecting to the "Weather Underground," a service provided by the University of Michigan's College of Engineering. The Weather Underground has a menu system that's almost easier to use than your automatic teller machine. You can find information such as your local weather, snow ski reports for some parts of the country, earthquake reports for other parts, and hurricane reports (so the Southern folks won't feel left out).

Sometimes when you login to another system, you'll be asked about your terminal type. In most cases, you can say you're emulating a "VT-100" (or something similar) terminal, and you'll do just fine. Some resources, such as online library catalogs, are running on IBM mainframes, however, so you might have to use a different version of Telnet called **tn3270** (if it exists on your system) in order to

emulate an IBM 3270 terminal. It works similarly, though
the keys may not correspond exactly to what you're used
to; just substitute *tn3270* for *telnet.*

Let Me Outa Here!!!

Why is it so hard to say goodbye? Sometimes the biggest
problem new users have using publicly available services is
getting out of them without shutting down the computer.
When you're remotely logged into another computer,
everything you type is being sent to the remote system for
execution. There are two ways to exit a system. One way is
simply to logout of the service. Unfortunately, there's no
standard "let me go" command. The best advice is to carefully read any instructions that show up when you login to
a system. If the screen doesn't tell you anything, try one of
these commands: *exit, quit, logout, leave, bye, goodbye, ciao,
disconnect, CTRL-D, CTRL-Z.*

   If you still can't exit, then you can terminate the session
by signaling your *local* telnet program that you wish to
quit. Using a special "escape" character or command allows you to temporarily suspend your telnet session, and
you're "brought back to reality" to a telnet prompt (usually
`telnet>`) on your home system. The escape character can
vary, but on many systems it's a *CTRL-].* (Hold down the
control key and at the same time press the *]* key.) On some
systems, *CTRL-^* is used. You can then quit the telnet session
by typing **quit** at the telnet prompt.

ONLINE RESOURCES

The Weather Underground is neat, but it's just the tip of the
tornado! There's much, much more. We'll give you an idea
of the types of resources available and how to try some of
them out.

Online Library Catalogs

Some of the most common and most-often-mentioned

> **plokta** /plok'ta/ [Acronym for 'Press Lots Of Keys To Abort'] v. To press random keys in an attempt to get some response from the system. One might plokta when the abort procedure for a program is not known, or when trying to figure out if the system is just sluggish or really hung. Plokta can also be used while trying to figure out any unknown key sequence for a particular operation. Someone going into *plokta mode* usually places both hands flat on the keyboard and presses down, hoping for some useful response.
>
> Source: *The New Hacker's Dictionary,* edited by Eric S. Raymond, with assistance and illustrations by Guy L. Steele Jr. (Cambridge, Mass.: The MIT Press, 1991). Reprinted with permission.

Internet resources are the online library catalogs. At least 500 catalogs are accessible via the Internet, mostly at academic organizations all over the world. Most don't allow you to look at or transfer entire online books; they just let you review bibliographic records. You can peruse a certain library's collection, verify a citation or reference, or see if a book is checked out or if it's available through the interlibrary loan system. Online library catalogs, by the way, are usually open all day and all night!

Some online catalogs offer more than just bibliographic records. For example, to explore the UHCARL Library System at the University of Hawaii, Manoa, type:

```
telnet starmaster.uhcc.hawaii.edu
```

At the `enter class` prompt, type **lib**. Select **5** for VT-100 emulation. Wander through the menus. (See if *this* book has been checked out.) Items of interest include an index of Hawaiian sheet music and the 1992 edition of the Hawaii Data Book.

Some online library catalogs even offer access to online encyclopedias! So you could connect to one of these services and learn all about the endangered gorillas of Rwanda. Not

> "The most important piece of information for poten-
> tial users to know is that the resource is *gigantic* and is
> growing larger. If it were an eggplant, we'd be in real
> danger."
>
> —Steve Cavrak, University of Vermont

every service offered in the menus may be available to
outside users. Some, such as online encyclopedias, may be
limited to registered users because of licensing restrictions.

Bulletin Board Systems

Bulletin board systems (BBSs) on the Internet are a lot like
the electronic bulletin boards that you can dial into using a
modem. Most BBSs offer a menu of services. Some provide
conferencing capabilities, while others provide "read-only"
information, similar to regular bulletin boards at a library
where information is tacked up for everyone to read and
taken down when it's no longer relevant. SpaceMet
Internet is an online bulletin board at the University of
Massachusetts (Amherst) for educators and students interested in space-related topics:

```
telnet spacemet.phast.umass.edu
```

Freenets.   Freenets are community-based bulletin board
systems with email, information services, interactive communications, and conferencing. Freenets are funded and
operated by individuals and volunteers—in one sense, like
public television. They're part of the National Public Telecommunication Network (NPTN), an organization based in
Cleveland, Ohio, devoted to making computer telecommunication and networking services as freely available as
public libraries. The Freenet concept is catching on, and
they're opening up in more and more areas. Access is
usually by a local dial phone call using a modem, but a good
number have also connected to the Internet.

The Cleveland Freenet, operated by Case Western Reserve University Community Laboratory, is one of the best-known. It's organized almost like a campus or old-fashioned downtown. Thousands of people access this system each day, chatting with each other and visiting the courthouse, the library, the arts building, or the community center. Academy One, an innovative educational resource—a sort of electronic schoolhouse—is available. There's also an online version of *USA Today* and lots of other interesting and useful information. Want to try it? Here's the command:

```
telnet freenet-in-a.cwru.edu
```

If you're a first-time user and don't have an account, you can demo the system by selecting the *visitor* login choice. From there you can apply for an account free of charge, if you wish, or you can just explore the system. The Cleveland Freenet can also be accessed via dialup phone, at (216) 368-3888.

Campus-Wide Information System. Also known as CWIS, campus-wide information services are popping up at universities and other types of institutions all over the world—many in the United States and others in Canada, Australia, and the United Kingdom. Usually menu-based, CWIS are digital kiosks that provide campus-specific information such as event calendars, phone and email directories, newsletters, restaurant guides, local weather, available jobs, athletic and cultural events, and course catalogs. While much of the information may not be of interest to outsiders, some of the services do provide links to useful databases and online library catalogs. Also, these systems may be a good place to look for email addresses. A popular CWIS is Cornell's, which you can access by using the following command:

```
telnet cuinfo.cornell.edu 300
```

Some items of interest on this system include Uncle Ezra,

Reach Out, Australia

People take pity on poor graduate students all over the world. Joanne Smedly, an information services librarian at Australian National University, got a request from a postgraduate student who needed to track down a Ph.D. thesis that had just been completed at Cornell. He asked Joanne if she could get some information that hadn't shown up in *Dissertation Abstracts.* "I got into the CWIS for Cornell," Joanne said, where she discovered that although the faculty supervisor didn't have an email address, there was someone in the next office who did. She emailed the neighbor and got a response within a few days. "I felt at the time this was a nice lateral approach to the problem! Given the postgrad had no money to telephone and no computer on his own desk, I thought I would try!"

an electronic counselor (you'll have to see it to understand it!); directories of students, faculty, and staff; job listings; descriptions of current patents held by Cornell; campus groups' newsletters; and local weather and ski reports. See the appendix for instructions on getting a regularly updated list of CWIS sites.

Databases and Data Archives

You want data? The Internet's got data! Molecular biology, astronomy, law, medicine, agriculture—you name it, it's probably accessible and searchable via remote login. For instance, PEN Pages, provided by the College of Agricultural Sciences at Pennsylvania State University, has news articles, fact sheets, and reports on agricultural and consumer topics. If you need to check the market price for pork bellies or pineapples, learn how to measure growth of your Guernsey heifers, or find out when and where the next Corn Silage Production Meeting is held, this is the place to look.

```
telnet psupen.psu.edu
```

Login with the two-letter abbreviation for your state (i.e., *TX* for Texas, *NH* for New Hampshire), or *WORLD*, if you're outside the United States; no password is needed.

One of the more esoteric online databases is the Dartmouth Dante database, providing online, full text access to Dante's *La Commedia*, along with centuries of commentary. To access it:

```
telnet lib.dartmouth.edu
```

At the first prompt, type **connect dante**.

Supercomputers

We would be remiss if we didn't mention access to supercomputer centers. After all, they are part of the reason the Internet exists. The ARPANET provided researchers scattered across the country access to expensive computational facilities, and the NSFNET backbone was originally built to connect supercomputer centers. Supercomputers are being used to do more than just develop and crack encryption and security codes. Now they're also handling more mundane things such as predicting the weather and studying the environment. Access via remote login is still mostly limited to scientists and researchers; an account and a reason to use them is needed. It's nice to know, however, that they're around and that, if you have a reason, you can access them.

Menu-based Systems

We've covered a few popular resources, but there is much, much more. It's hard to remember *what* services are available, let alone *where* they are! If you have direct access to the Internet, you can use menu systems that will organize

SAMPLER OF ONLINE DATABASES AND SERVICES

The Federal Information Exchange (FEDIX) service provides information for colleges, universities, and other research organizations. Telnet to host *fedix.fie.com*, login **fedix.**

National Bureau of Time service will give you the exact time. Use telnet to connect to *india.colorado.edu 13*.

GTE Contel DUAT System allows pilots to file flight plans and get weather briefings. Two addresses: *duat.contel.com* is for pilots, and *duats.contel.com* is for pilots and nonpilots.

the many databases, online library catalogs, bulletin board systems, and campus-wide information services by subject, type of service, or geographic location. You won't have to remember host names or port numbers; these menu-based systems will make the connections for you. Two information resource access systems that you may hear about are: Libtel, developed by Dan Mahoney at the University of New Mexico, and Hytelnet, developed by Peter Scott at the University of Saskatchewan.

The programs are freely available (via anonymous FTP), and they will run on your computer. (See the appendix for information on where to get them.) There are also public demo systems that you can telnet to. Check out a version of Libtel, running on the *bbs.oit.unc.edu* computer; login as **bbs** and work through the opening dialog to apply for an account. The Hytelnet demo is running on *access.usask.ca* login as **hytelnet**. Another popular menu-based service that you can access via remote login is WUGATE, a library/database access system that is run by the Washington University in St. Louis. The host is *wugate.wustl.edu*; the login name is **library**.

TRANSFERRING INFORMATION

Imagine that you're creating an important report at your personal workstation. You want to print it out, but you don't have a printer. So you copy the document onto a floppy, put on your Keds, and run down the hall to load the floppy at the nearest workstation-printer site. This process is known as **file transfer,** because the report is being transferred to another computer. Now, if both computers were on the Internet, you could have transferred this file in a matter of seconds using the file transfer capability. Instead of sending the file through the slower "SneakerNet," you could have sent it over the electronic highway. In short, the file transfer capability gives you the ability to copy files from one computer to another.

What Is a File?

A file can be anything. It can be a document you create in your PC's word processor. It can be a spreadsheet or a software program. It can be a picture, or even music. Or it can be ASCII (American Standard Code for Information Interchange) text, which is just plain vanilla text with no formatting codes such as boldface or underlining.

Many of the documents are just text, useful (and readable by humans) no matter what computer or software you're using. You should be aware, however, that some of the files you transfer won't mean anything to the system you're on. A word processor document—let's say, one that was prepared by Microsoft Word—has special codes within the document that signal the program to "make this word bold" or "use the Times font." Obviously, this file won't mean much to you if you don't own the Microsoft Word application.

Similarly, a file can be a software application. Not all software will "run" or work on every computer. In fact, it's safe to say that there isn't one piece of software that will work on every type of computer. A Macintosh program won't run directly on a PC, and vice versa. Similarly, a program created for the VMS operating system won't run on a UNIX system. (VMS and UNIX are operating systems, just like DOS is an operating system for PCs.)

File Transfer Clarified

Many people get file transfer and remote login confused—
an easy enough thing to do. Both applications allow you to
connect to other computers and obtain information, but file
transfer is a more specific and straightforward tool. Its main
mission is to transfer files between computers. You're not
actually interactively querying another computer's database or using a service to find out any information.

There are also similarities and differences between file
transfer and electronic mail. Email is used for transferring
personal messages, although you can send and receive
information in the form of files, too. You wouldn't use file
transfer to deliver personal messages, but if you and another
person need to transfer a file—say a text document—back
and forth, then electronic mail will work just fine. Indeed,
in most cases this is probably preferable, because you don't
want to give another person your username and password.
Two warnings, however: Some computers cannot handle
extremely long email messages. If your file is very large, you
may need to send it in smaller sections. Some email systems
can also throw extra characters into your text, but file
transfer guarantees integrity.

If the file is a nontext file, like a software program, then
it's almost always better to transfer it by using the Internet
file transfer tool. As mentioned in Chapter 3, you can send
text files only using the current commonly available email
technology. If you want to send a nontext file via email, it
is necessary first to convert it to text, using an encoding
program. Since this process requires several extra steps (it
has to be decoded upon arrival, too), it may just be simpler
to use file transfer rather than email.

How File Transfer Works

Using the file transfer capability on the Internet is fairly
straightforward. The protocol is called File Transfer Protocol
(FTP). On many systems, the actual program that you will
use is called *ftp*, which stands for file transfer program. FTP

allows you to connect to another computer and perform certain actions, such as listing the files in a directory and copying files back and forth between both systems.

To start a session, type **ftp** *host-name*. (Or you can also use the **ftp** command by itself, at which time you'll be put into the command interpreter, which waits for more instructions from you. The **open** *host-name* command will establish a transfer connection.) You should be prompted for your username and password on the remote system, just as in the telnet process. Once you've identified yourself to the remote system, you'll most likely see a prompt that looks like this: ftp>

When you use FTP, be sure to check local system documentation for more information. It will tell you about the many other commands and things you can do, as well as any system-specific characteristics you should know about. Keep in mind that most of the following commands will tell you information about and perform actions on the *remote* system. For example, you can find out what files are in the remote directory using the command **dir** (for "directory") or **ls** (for "list"). You can change to another directory where other files are stored using the command **cd** *directory-name* ("change directory"). To go back up the directory ladder to the parent directory, use the **cdup** command. If you don't know which directory you're in, the **pwd** ("print working directory") command will tell you.

Now, if the "changing directories" part of this confuses you, then you need to understand that directories in computers can be organized similarly to folders in a filing cabinet. A directory is basically an electronic folder with files and perhaps other folders in it, and when you change directories, you're just opening up a new folder. Once you're "in" the right directory on the remote system, you can do several things, two of which are *getting* a file (or files) and *putting* a file (or files). To download or transfer a file from the remote system to your local computer, use the **get** *filename* command. To upload or put a local file on the remote system, use the **put** *filename* command. You can

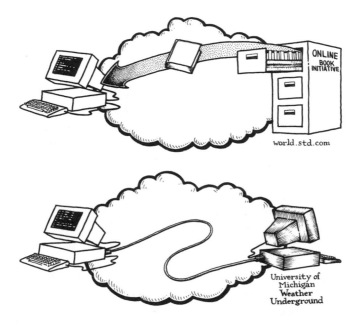

world.std.com

University of
Michigan
Weather
Underground

File transfer (above) lets you move files between computers. Remote login (below) lets you interact with another Internet computer's services.

always get help by typing **help** (for a list of commands) or **help** *command*. In fact, you should probably check out the help screens on any system when you are using it for the first time. When you finish transferring files, you can close the connection and exit by typing either **bye** or **quit**.

Many of the public archive sites run the UNIX operating system, so if you're familiar with that, then the listing **dir** produces will make sense. If you're not, it may help to know that the UNIX file system is a hierarchical directory structure similar to that of a DOS or Macintosh computer. Also, UNIX is case-sensitive, so if a filename is shown in lower case, then you must type it in lower case. (A good rule is to *always* type the instructions or filename exactly as shown.) Chapter 5 will tell you a bit about UNIX commands. Following is a sample listing of a directory on an anonymous FTP host that runs UNIX:

```
-rw-r--r--  1 tracy   ftp      198 Apr 10 13:16 README
dr-xr-xr-x  2 root    bin      512 Apr  1  1991 bin
dr-xr-xr-x  2 root    bin      512 Apr  1  1991 etc
-rw-r--r--  1 tracy   ftp    88349 Aug  2 15:26 glossary
dr-xrwxr-x 14 ftp     ftp      512 Jul 23 09:10 pub
```

In this example, the filenames are on the far right. On the far left are the permission and file type specifications. The letter *d* in the first column indicates that the entry is a directory, so *bin, etc,* and *pub* are directories. The file creation date and time are easy to spot: *README* was created or modified on April 10 at 1:16 p.m. And finally, another thing you should notice is the number immediately to the left of the date: the size of the file in bytes. The glossary file is 88,349 bytes, which is fairly large. Because it's so easy to transfer files, you may find that you can fill up your disk space quickly, so you'll need to get a good file management system going. Remember to delete the files you don't need and to compress the ones you want to keep.

Publicly Accessible Files

The transfer of publicly available information is one of the most widespread uses of the file transfer capability on the Internet. Many of the organizations connected to the Internet provide openly accessible file transfer sites with information that anyone can obtain (or *get*). Files are stored in "open" areas of computers, and you can access them by using the file transfer program to connect to those systems. A file that is "available via anonymous FTP" is publicly available, and you can connect to a public archive computer and use the file transfer program to copy it to your own system.

Remember that you need a login name and password to be allowed into a computer. For publicly accessible files, the login name is **anonymous** and the password can be

> "Libraries are the last democratic educational institu-
> tion . . . the most important and democratic source of
> information . . . and the last refuge of those without
> modems."
>
> —Gloria Steinem, speech at the American Library Association in July
> 1992.

anything, although it's a good idea to type your email
address. (Sometimes **guest** is the specific password required.) Once you master spelling *anonymous*, you can roam
around the public storage areas on computers on the
Internet just as you explore public libraries.

Not every computer on the Internet makes public file
storage areas available, but at least 1300 known systems
offer gigabytes and gigabytes of information. These sites are
making available electronic books, public domain software,
and graphic images—lots of amusing, useful, and interesting
stuff. Check the appendix for information on obtaining a
list of anonymous FTP sites.

Navigating around different computer public storage
areas takes some practice. As we've mentioned before, there
are different kinds of computers out there, and some present
their electronic folders a bit differently. Many systems provide README files that explain what files are available or
anything you might need to know about the collection of
files. You simply transfer the README file: **get README**.
(There's no standard name for an information file; they may
be called *00README*, or *readme, READ.me, INFO, INDEX*, etc.
You can usually tell what file will provide information when
you get a directory listing.)

Let's transfer an electronic book, *Aesop's Fables*. This
online volume is made available through Project Gutenberg, a volunteer organization dedicated to making electronic texts freely available. In addition to *Aesop's Fables*,
Project Gutenberg has *Moby Dick,* Roget's *Thesaurus, The Book*

of Mormon, The Bible, Shakespeare's plays and sonnets, *Song of Hiawatha, Through the Looking Glass,* a Webster's dictionary, and *The CIA World Factbook*—to name just a few—so you may want to "root around" when you get on this system.

We happen to know that *Aesop's Fables* is available via anonymous FTP on the computer *mrcnext.cso.uiuc.edu,* in the directory *gutenberg/etext91,* with the filename *aesop11.txt.* In this example, we won't show a directory listing (using the *dir* command), but you can use that command to see what other files are available. If you wish to rename the file as you're transferring it to your system, the command is **get** *remote-file new-file-name.* Here's what you'd see on your screen (the commands you would type are shown in bold):

```
ftp mrcnext.cso.uiuc.edu
Connected to mrcnext.cso.uiuc.edu.
220 mrcnext.cso.uiuc.edu FTP server (Version
     5.20 (NeXT 1.0) Sun Nov 11, 1990) ready.
Name (mrcnext.cso.uiuc.edu:tracy): anonymous
Password (mrcnext.cso.uiuc.edu:anonymous):
331 Guest login ok, send ident as password.
230 Guest login ok, access restrictions apply.
ftp> cd gutenberg/etext91
250 CWD command successful.
ftp> get aesop11.txt
200 PORT command successful.
150 Opening ASCII mode data connection for
     aesop11.txt (241062 bytes).
226 Transfer complete.
local: aesop11.txt remote: aesop11.txt
246283 bytes received in 3.6 seconds (68
     Kbytes/s)
ftp> quit
221 Goodbye.
```

Non-Text Information

The above directions work fine if you're transferring text files. When you fire up an FTP session, the system assumes that you are transferring ASCII text files unless you specify otherwise. But if you plan on transferring software or "unreadable" files (meaning files that have been encoded to mean something only to a particular computer or program), you'll need to tell the computers that you're doing a **binary transfer.** Files that have been **compressed** are binary files, as are software programs. A compressed file is basically "dehydrated," or squeezed, to conserve disk space and also to make the transfer time faster. Type **binary** <RETURN> before you type **get** or **put** to transfer a file to tell the system that you're moving a compressed, or non-text, file. Typing **ascii** will put you back in text mode.

Obtaining Software

Need some software? Software archives are all over the Internet. The Washington University Public Domain Archives is a great place to start, with a boatload of public domain and shareware software for the Amiga, Apple II, Atari, CP/M, DOS, GNU, Macintosh, Sun, TeX, UNIX, VMS, and X Windows systems. There's so much on this system that it's advisable to obtain any README files in each directory to learn about what's available when you're exploring. If you want to check out this system, type the **ftp wuarchive.wustl.edu** command, login as **anonymous**, and use your email address as a password. (But don't forget to specify *binary* transfer for software!) Before you stock up on software, read the section on security in Chapter 5.

File Formats

As we said earlier, certain files work only on certain computers, so it's good to have a little knowledge of the types of files, how to know which is which, and what programs, if any, you'll need to use the files. Macintosh programs are sometimes in the BinHex (ASCII) format. Once downloaded and un-BinHexed, the files will most likely have to be uncompressed. Because PC files and programs are usually in binary format, they will almost always have to be un-compressed with a utility like PKZIP or StuffIt after being

---

From Russia with Byte

Worried about gainful employment for all those Russian scientists and computer types, now that they're not doing arms development? Dave Hughes was looking for a way to develop a universal graphics/telecommunication package for education—and to make it inexpensive enough for schools to buy. No funding on these shores, so he hooked up with some Russian computer scientists and hired them to write the software. The Russians get a very capitalistic piece of potential sales and are paid in hard currency. So what's the Internet connection? Hughes and friends are in the United States, the programmers live in Moscow. They've never even met. And everything— software standards, technical documentation, general articles, sample software, code models—travels the Internet.

Derived from a posting by Dave Hughes on the Consortium for School Networking Discussion Forum List<COSNDISC@bitnic.bitnet>.

---

downloaded. A document available via anonymous FTP explains most file compression, archiving, and text-binary formats and tells where you can get software to convert these various formats. This regularly updated document is maintained by David Lemson and can be obtained via anonymous FTP from *ftp.cso.uiuc.edu*, in the directory *doc/pcnet*, filename *compression*. The chart on p. 99 shows some of the more common file types you'll see, the programs they work with, and how you should transfer (ASCII or binary mode) each of them.

Obtaining Information via Electronic Mail

If you don't have direct access to the Internet, are you forever cut off from publicly available files? Take heart, there are other ways to get files. If you are in a situation

ONLINE INFORMATION SAMPLER

You can get almost any type of information on the Internet. Here are some examples of items currently available:

- Supreme Court rulings, via anonymous FTP to *ftp.cwru.edu*, directory *hermes*. See the *INFO* file and the various README files for more information.
- Lyrics to popular songs, interviews with musicians, sound samplers, and other musically related information, available from the Lyric/Music Server on *cs.uwp.edu*, directory *pub/music*.
- Sound Archive of digitized sounds for the Mac and PC, available on the host *ccb.ucsf.edu*, in the *Pub/Sound_list* directory. See the *=readme=* file. Note that you have to type those directories and filenames exactly as shown (including upper and lower case).
- Glasnost Archives containing sample pages from an exhibit of the Library of Congress' newly opened Soviet archives, available via anonymous FTP to *seq1.loc.gov*, directory *pub/soviet.archive*.

where you can't interactively use FTP, then you might want to check out the alternatives explained in this section.

Using what's called an *info-server*, *archive-server*, or an *email-server*, you can get publicly accessible files (normally available via anonymous FTP on the Internet) essentially by placing an "order" for a file (using special commands) in an email message. (One command that should always work is **help**.) The message is sent to the address of a server that processes the order and emails the requested files back to you within a few minutes or, usually, by the next day. That's all there is to it. If you're interested in knowing which computers offer publicly available files via email, check the appendix for information about how to get a regularly updated list.

The National Science Foundation Network Service Center (NNSC) provides an Info-Server for documents available via anonymous FTP on *nnsc.nsf.net*. You can test

Common File Formats on the Internet

Computer	Program/type	File Extension	Transfer Method
Mac	MacBinary	.bin	binary (Encoded)
Mac	Compact Pro	.cpt	binary (Compressed)
Mac	BinHex 4.0	.hqx	ASCII (Encoded)
Mac	self extracting	.sea	binary (Mac Application)
Mac	StuffIt	.sit	binary (Compressed)
PC	ARC, PKPAK	.arc	binary (Compressed)
PC	ARJ	.arj	binary (Compressed)
PC	LHArc	.lzh	binary (Compressed)
PC	PAK	.pak	binary (Compressed)
PC	Soundblaster	.voc	binary (Sound)
PC	WAVE	.wav	binary (Sound)
PC	PKZIP/InfoZIP	.zip	binary (Compressed)
PC	zoo	.zoo	binary (Compressed)
UNIX	compress & uncompress	.Z	binary (Compressed)
UNIX	tar	.tar	binary (Multiple files)
Any	PostScript	.ps	ASCII (Page Description)
Any	GIF	.gif	binary (Graphics)
Any	text	.txt	ASCII (text)

this out by sending email to *info-server@nnsc.nsf.net*. In the body of the message (you don't have to worry about what's in the Subject: field), type the following text:

```
request: info
topic: help
```

A help file will be sent, explaining how to use the Info-Server. You might want to get a Hypercard *Tour of the Internet*; instructions are listed in the *help* file. This tour is also available via anonymous FTP to the host *nnsc.nsf.net*, directory *internet-tour*. See the *Internet-Tour-README* file.

FTP-by-Email Server.   The Info-Server directions above work only if the computer that has your desired file supports an email server. Unfortunately, such services don't exist on every computer offering anonymous FTP access. Some computers, however, will act as general purpose email/FTP translation servers. You can send orders for *any* publicly available files, no matter what computer they're on. The FTP-by-email server will try to transfer the files from the computers they reside on, and will then email them to you.

   One FTP by mail server is *ftpmail@pa.dec.com*. Send an email message to that address, with a one-line message in the body: **help**. (Don't worry about the Subject; anything will do.) You will be sent a help file telling you what commands to use to obtain files. Another server is BITFTP, named because it processes file requests from BITNET users. If you're on BITNET, send email (command **help** initially) to *BITFTP@PUCC* or *bitftp@pucc.princeton.edu*. You should receive a help file explaining how to use BITFTP.

FINDING RESOURCES AND FILES

So many resources and public archives are available that we can't even begin to cover everything, and people all over the world are constantly cooking up interesting new offerings. There is no *one* Internet resource "card catalog" because of the difficulty in cataloging everything. Consider, for example, the following variety of topics:

- The radar summary weather maps generated hourly for the United States (anonymous FTP *vmd.cso.uiuc.edu*, directory *wx*).
- A geographic name server (use the command **telnet martini.eecs.umich. edu 3000;** type **?** for help).
- A collection of public domain Macintosh software (anonymous FTP *sumex-aim.stanford.edu*).
- Technion University's (Israel) Library Catalogs (use the command **telnet lib.technion.ac.il;** login as **ALEPH).**

- A public file archive of history documents (anonymous FTP *ra.msstate.edu*, directory *pub/docs/history*).
- A smorgasbord of electronic books, made available by various groups.

There *are* lots of resource directories, guides, lists of public FTP sites, and lists of online library catalogs that can help show you the way to some important resources. Usually they're maintained by volunteers and made available without cost via anonymous FTP, posted regularly to certain mailing lists and newsgroups, or in hardcopy form for a nominal price. The appendix lists the more popular guides. Sometimes, however, you just have to resort to learning about new resources through mailing lists and USENET postings or by word of mouth. Or you may read a newsletter article about the Internet and find out about a new server. This is true discovery—which is fun—but it makes you feel as though you're missing out if you aren't reading email or news in the right places or if you're not talking to the right people.

Advanced Information Discovery and Retrieval Tools

Online lists and guides are useful for reading about interesting online services but there are so many resources and information archives available that it's hard to keep these guides up to date. They can also be difficult to search if you've got something particular in mind that you want to know about.

Fortunately, there are electronic tools springing up that will help you search and browse documents, retrieve information on certain subjects, and locate resources of interest to you. Some of the best known and most used are archie, WAIS, Gopher, and World Wide Web. These tools each provide a single interface into the hundreds of disparate services and databases on the Internet, offering easier ways to search or browse them. In other words, you don't have to remember computer names, port numbers, or directory structures, or learn lots of new interfaces. In some cases they can even establish links and relationships between other tools and services, helping you to find information more easily.

Clients and Servers

To comprehend how these advanced applications work, you need to understand a fundamental networking concept: the client/server model. In general, **clients** are applications that run on your own computer, taking advantage of its features. A graphical interface, for instance, allows you to use your mouse instead of typing in commands. A client hides many of the network details from you, including computer names, ports, and commands, and it obtains its information from servers. **Servers** are just programs running on computers that are reachable via the network. They know where the data and documents are and take care of servicing client queries.

Client programs that hide networking details are nice for novice users who don't know a lot about how the Internet works or what commands to use. Unfortunately, the client/server model requires a *direct* network connection to the Internet. So if you're sitting at home with just a microcomputer, modem, and terminal emulation software, you may not be able to partake of these powerful applications right away. If, however, you can remotely login to computers on the Internet, there are some simple, terminal-based interfaces that you can use. They're not as friendly and easy to use as their graphical client counterparts, but they'll give you an idea of what they can do. Information on how to obtain the free client programs for all of these applications is listed in the appendix.

All of this talk may sound a bit intimidating, but we did call these *advanced* tools. You definitely will have to spend a little time—and probably endure some frustration—to learn your way around. If you have a real need, or if you're

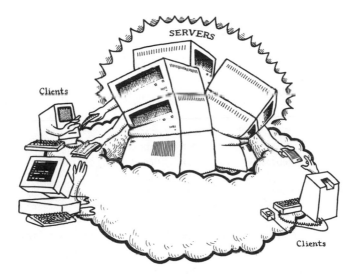

Client programs hide network details from you. Server programs find Internet resources and deliver them to your computer.

just an incorrigible information junkie, the trouble will definitely be worth it.

Archie

Let's start with the easiest to use and most readily understood application: **archie** (derived from the word *archive*) is an online file-finding utility developed at the McGill University (Montreal) School of Computer Science. If you've ever looked high and low for a file on your microcomputer's hard disk, you'll understand the usefulness of this tool. About 1300 (and increasing) known public sites are providing access to files via anonymous FTP. Trying to figure out where a particular document or archive is located on the Internet is like looking for the proverbial needle in a digital haystack.

The way it works is simple. The archie system maintains a database of all the names of files stored at known public archive sites. A user can search this database by using a client program, by remotely logging into an archie server

Public archie Servers

Country/State	archie Server Name
Australia	*archie.au*
Canada	*archie.mcgill.ca*
Finland	*archie.funet.fi*
UK/Ireland	*archie.doc.ic.ac.uk*
Maryland	*archie.sura.net*
Nebraska	*archie.unl.edu*
New York	*archie.ans.net*
New Jersey	*archie.rutgers.edu*

computer, or by sending email (with commands) to the server. Quite a few server computers are scattered throughout the world, and users are requested to pick the one that's closest to them. If you're not sure where to go, you can log into the McGill server—**telnet quiche.cs.mcgill.ca**, login as **archie**. Once you're on, type **help** to get a list of commands. If you want to start searching for a file, simply type **prog** *filename*, where *filename* is the name of the file you're searching for. Archie will "think" for a while and then produce a list of every place that has a file by that name. You can then have this list sent to you via email by typing **mail** *your-email-address*. When you're done searching, just type **exit** to get back to home base.

If you want to search for public file sites where recipes are stored, for example, telnet to the nearest archie host, login **archie**, type **prog recipes**, and sit back for awhile. Archie will spit out about 220 places where recipes are stored. You can then look through this list for a file that sounds appealing and FTP a new healthy or exotic recipe that you can retrieve and try out for dinner.

If your Internet access is limited and you can't telnet to an archie server, you can access archie via email. Basically, you send commands in an email message to an archie server and the results are emailed back to you. To test this out, send a message to **archie**@*nearest-archie-server* (see table on page 104), with the command **help** in the body of the message. A description of the basic commands will be sent to you. You can then use the "FTP by Email Servers" described earlier to obtain the files you want.

Wide Area Information Servers

Archie will tell you *where* a file is, based on a name that you give it, but it can't help you search for information based on what's *in* the file. That's a job for an application called **Wide Area Information Servers** (**WAIS**, pronounced "ways"). WAIS was conceived by Brewster Kahle and developed by Dow Jones, Thinking Machines, Apple Computer, and KPMC Peat Marwick as a joint project. WAIS allows you to search for information in databases located on server computers. How does it work? Think of WAIS as a sort of electronic reference librarian. When you ask it where you can get information on a certain subject, it searches databases and returns documents it thinks will help you. Now, the servers don't actually *understand* your question; they simply look for documents that contain the words and phrases you used. The documents can be pictures and sound as well as text.

The WAIS system is very powerful and covers a lot of territory. At least 400 databases (more being made available every day) are on server computers all over the world. Here's just a sampling of the information you have access to: poetry, *The Bible*, Educational Resources Information Center (ERIC), the current weather, molecular biology, recipes, zip codes, science fiction reviews, Roget's *Thesaurus*, agricultural market news, documents about the Internet, a number of organization phone books, and a variety of USENET news archives. You can try out a simple WAIS terminal interface by remotely logging into *quake.think.com*, username **wais**. While this interface is not as user-friendly as a graphical client interface, it does let you check out the system to see exactly what databases are available.

Is There a Swimming Pool
in the Kremlin?

A group of reference librarians at a major university library (which shall remain nameless) were a bit skeptical when a WAIS terminal was installed at their reference desk. Not that they were computerphobic. Far from it, they just felt they were already masters of the best research tools available. So someone posed the question, "Is there a swimming pool in the Kremlin?" Well, in this post-glasnost era, certainly we should be able to find out.

The reference librarians scurried off to their favorite research mines—some to the card catalog, some to Dialog, some to the periodical indexes. The WAIS wizard worked quietly at his terminal. Within ten minutes, he'd found several citations and one whole article about a retired member of the Red Guard who swam every day, just outside the Kremlin walls. More than half an hour after he'd finished, the librarians straggled back. A few had struck out. A couple had a few cold leads, and one had, with a lot more work, located the same article in about quadruple the time it took on WAIS. Think they were convinced?

Gopher

Gopher is an application that organizes access to Internet resources using a uniform interface that's simple to understand and easy to use. It provides smooth passage into other computers, allowing you to browse and search documents, and links you to resources and databases such as USENET news, online library catalogs, and Campus Wide Information Servers. So while you're "sniffing" around "Gopherspace," you may not know it, but you're actually doing things like transferring files, changing directories, telneting to computers, and querying servers (including archie and

Public Telnet Gopher Sites

Hostname	Login Id	Geographical Area
consultant.micro.umn.edu	**gopher**	North America
gopher.uiuc.edu	**gopher**	North America
gopher.uwp.edu	**gopher**	North America
panda.uiowa.edu	**panda**	North America
info.anu.edu.au	**info**	Australia
gdunix.gd.chalmers.se	**gopher**	Sweden

WAIS) all over the world. You can get an idea of how gopher works by remotely logging into one of the public gopher telnet sites. It's recommended that you choose one that's closest to you.

World Wide Web

World Wide Web (**WWW** or **W³**) is a browsing and searching system that allows you to explore a seemingly unlimited worldwide digital "web" of information. The system links related documents using a very powerful concept called **hypertext.** Basically, almost every piece of information you look at provides you with pointers, or links, which you can follow to other documents on the same or related subject. You can travel the strands of the web, locating information of interest to you. You don't have to know where anything is, for a particular journey may present you with information from many different servers. WWW does more than just let you browse; it also allows you to search for key words in certain documents. You can try the simple line mode browser by telnet-ing to *info.cern.ch*. It's not as sophisticated as the client browsers are, but you can get a basic idea of how it works.

The resources we've described in this chapter only skim the surface of what's available on the Internet. Once you've mastered remote login and file transfer, you'll be able to use the Internet to track down a single fact or expand your horizons with masses of information. With the guideposts we've given you, you'll be able to locate even more resources to explore.

As you roam the Internet, you'll definitely get the sense that there's a culture and a shared history—things that people just "know." So that you don't feel left out, Chapter 5 will give the flavor of the Internet culture, tell you some of what's gone on before you made the scene, and give you some "insider" information about security, UNIX commands, and where in the network world you can go to get help.

Chapter 5

INTERNET IN-THE-KNOW GUIDE

*N*ow that you've learned what you can do on the Internet and a bit about how it works, it's time to cover a few "Advanced Internet Topics." The Internet is more than just how-to. It has its own culture, its own myths and legends. There are fantasy games on the Internet that become a world unto themselves for many of the players. You should know, too, about the organizations dedicated to the Internet and to network users. And there are some technical niceties—such as directory services and advanced methods for finding email addresses and UNIX commands—that you can master if you're willing. Technical necessities, like computer security, are a must-read. A final section gives some direction for times when you need additional information or help with an Internet problem.

Put a few million people together anywhere, even in electronic cyberspace, and they'll develop some kind of culture—a fabric of shared experiences, shared recreation, shared fears, shared rules of behavior—that makes them all feel part of a community. We talked about the Internet's formal and informal codes of conduct in Chapter 3. Now it's time to learn about some of the less tangible aspects of the Internet culture, the 'Net legends, and the notable—and notorious—subculture of network games.

LEGENDS ON THE INTERNET

Probably everyone knows at least one story that qualifies as an "urban legend"—a story that, while it may have started with a grain of truth, has been embroidered and retold until it has passed into the realm of myth. It's an interesting phenomenon that these stories get spread so far and so fast—and so often. Urban legends never die; they all just seem to end up on the Internet! You won't be on the Internet long before you start seeing references to these legends. Experienced Internet users have seen some of these old chestnuts come around regularly for years.

The Infamous Modem Tax

The FCC Modem Tax Scare is a classic example of an Internet legend that refuses to die. Several years ago, a proposal surfaced in Washington to put a telecommunications tax on modems. The tax was quickly squashed in a congressional committee, and it was not—repeat *not*—under reconsideration at the time this book was published. But you wouldn't know that from some users of the Internet. The scare resurfaces continually on the networks, riling new users at the prospect that their new-found electronic freedom is about to be taxed. The story just keeps on rolling. In one recent email exchange, fresh from the Internet, the story and the original (and *undated*) letters were forwarded, once again, to a user group with 40 members scattered all over the state of Texas. How far it was forwarded from here is anyone's guess.

The FCC story is essentially innocuous, though its constant recycling through the Internet wastes people's time, as well as network resources. It has also created a "cry wolf" situation, and if another modem tax ever *is* proposed, it will certainly be harder to mobilize the opposition. Imagine the damage, though, of a malicious rumor or flat-out lie, broadcast around the world again and again. After you imagine it, promise you'll think twice before you forward anything, and check the facts before you do.

Get Well Cards Gone Amok

Back in the mid-eighties, a British seven-year-old named Craig Shergold was diagnosed as having an inoperable brain tumor. Craig wanted to set the Guinness record for receiving the most get-well cards, and his efforts got worldwide publicity, from mimeographed sheets to email pleas.

Craig is thirteen now, and he's doing just fine; his brain tumor was successfully treated. He did set the Guinness record for get-well cards in 1989 and has gotten more than thirty million cards to date. That's the good news.

Incredibly, however, the Craig Shergold story keeps circulating on the Internet, as fresh as the day it started. Sometimes it mutates into requests for postcards or business cards, but otherwise the story is the same. The hospital where Craig was treated is still being buried with cards. The Shergolds (Craig's parents), the hospital, even Ann Landers have sent out pleas to stop them, but the story has taken on a life of its own, and the cards keep rolling in. In short, the situation has taken on a nightmarish quality for all involved. The hospital and post office, which have to cope with all of the cards, sell some to stamp collectors and paper recyclers. Guinness has discontinued the category to prevent anything like this from happening again.

So, if you see a plea on the network for cards for a little boy who's dying with a brain tumor, pass it up. And pass the word that Craig Shergold is doing just fine. No more cards, *please*!

The $250 Recipe

Another story that regularly makes the rounds is the $250 cookie recipe. As the story goes (in shortened form), a lady ate lunch at the restaurant in the Neiman-Marcus department store in Dallas and had their famous chocolate chip cookies for dessert. She thought they were so good that she asked for the recipe. Told that the recipe cost "two-fifty," she said, "Fine," and asked to have the charge added to her bill, which she paid with a Visa card. When her statement arrived a month later, the "two-fifty" was actually "two hundred and fifty" dollars! She tried in vain to get her money back, but the company wouldn't budge. So her revenge was to make sure that as many people as possible got a copy of the recipe.

Neiman-Marcus says it just plain never happened. They've never sold cookies in their restaurants; they don't even take Visa cards. Recipes from their restaurants are given out free to those who request them. The same tale has also circulated as the "Mrs. Fields Cookie Recipe." The story travels in low-tech circles as well as the Internet, recently surfacing as a bogus letter to Ann Landers. Try the cookie recipe(see p. 113); they're good! Just do your fellow users a favor and post the recipe on your refrigerator, not on the 'Net.

Chain Letters

Every now and then someone will get a chain letter and decide to send it to everyone they've ever known. Before copy machines, the letters had to be duplicated by hand or carbon copied in the typewriter. Electronic mail makes chain letters much easier—and just as annoying. Chain letters also violate every known acceptable use policy. So just don't send them.

GAMES

Just about every computer user has at least one game tucked away somewhere—the kind you play a bit surreptitiously when the boss isn't watching or you've got a bad case of writer's block. The Internet's no exception. There are shareware and freeware games you can download for your own computer, as well as game newsgroup discussions and email lists. Games are played on the Internet, too. There's the Trivia USENET Newsgroup, whose participants have gotten past naming all the seven dwarfs and have now moved on to higher-order thinking: naming all the characters in the Charlie Brown comic strip. Try the Weekly Trivia Contest on the USENET newsgroup *rec.games.trivia*.

The "$250" Cookie Recipe

2 cups of butter	1 teaspoon of salt
2 cups of sugar	2 teaspoons of baking
2 cups of brown	powder
sugar	2 teaspoons of baking soda
4 eggs	24 oz. of chocolate chips
2 teaspoons of	1 8 oz. Hershey bar, grated
vanilla	
4 cups of flour	3 cups of chopped nuts
5 cups of blended	
oatmeal*	

Cream butter, add both sugars. Add eggs and vanilla. Mix together with flour, oatmeal, salt, baking powder, and baking soda. Add chips, candy bar, and nuts. Roll into ball shape and place 2 inches apart on a cookie sheet. Bake for 6 to 10 minutes at 375 degrees F.

Yield: 112 cookies. The recipe can also be divided in half.

*Blended oatmeal: measure and blend in a blender to a fine powder.

As you might imagine, the "big" games on the Internet tend to match the network itself in scale and complexity, and they are a world and a culture unto themselves. Generally, the games—with names like Galactic Bloodshed, Empire, and Multi-User Dungeons (MUDs)—are adventure, role-playing games or simulations. Devotees call them "text-based virtual reality adventures." The games can feature fantasy combat, booby traps, and magic. Players interact in real time and can change the "world" in the game as they play it.

All of the games require the ability to use Telnet and demand an intense learning process to figure out all the characters and game idiosyncrasies, not to mention the rules. They can be extremely addictive; small-time players

The Man Behind the MUSE

Lately, armed with only my trusty modem, I have been wandering though cyberspace and spending time in a computer at MIT wherein lives a wonderful new world called MicroMUSE. I suppose MicroMUSE is one of those virtual reality things; I have come to distrust the phrase "virtual reality" the way, in another era, I came to distrust the word "lifestyle."

MUSE stands for Multi-User Simulation Environment; the environment in this case is a space station called Cyberion City. It's all text-based (there are no graphics) but then "Moby Dick" was a text-based adventure, too. It's a pretty vigorous form.

So fine; so fun. I was bumbling about talking to people, trying to learn more about the inner workings of MicroMUSE, and I was told that the very inventor of the entire system, Mr. MUSE himself, lived in the Bay Area. In Cyberion City, he's "Jin" (I'm "Scribe," by the way—yuck yuck); in real life he's Stan Lim and works at a Prominent Computer Company (herein-

(Continued)

may spend an hour or so a day. Some people literally spend all of their waking hours in the game. Many of the game players seem to feel the need to leave their mark on the game, and generations of game variations have evolved. Empire, for example, a military simulation written by Peter Langston, has five or six multi-player spinoffs and a single-player version. According to the *Hacker's Dictionary*, all of the empire games "are notoriously addictive."

In most games, new players take on a persona and then participate *in* the game. To quote from the Frequently Asked Questions document for Multi-User Dungeons, "You can walk around, chat with other characters, explore dangerous monster-infested areas, solve puzzles, and even create your

after PCC) on the Peninsula. We made a date; I drove down to see him.

Stan Lim is 23 years old, an electrical engineer at PCC; he has a small cubicle next to the machine shop. He invented MicroMUSE three years ago, when he was a senior at Cal State Fresno. It's all a labor of love, all volunteer; he's never received a penny from MicroMUSE; doesn't expect to. Does PCC know about MicroMUSE? "Oh, no," says Stan Lim. "I haven't told them. I don't know what they'd think."

He emphasizes that Cyberion City was a joint enterprise, its directors scattered all over the country. Only one, Barry Kort, a specialist in artificial intelligence working at MIT, is near the actual machine. And many of the key players in Cyberion City are even younger than Lim. "Our chief code hacker is 14," he says matter-of-factly. "Our youngest citizen is, let's see, 7 now. Kids really get into it fast; they make me feel old." For more information on MicroMUSE, log on to your local Internet host and send a message to *micro-muse-registration@chezmoto.ai.mit.edu*.

Source: Excerpted from a column by Jon Carroll that appeared in the *San Francisco Chronicle* on Tuesday, April 14, 1992. Reprinted with permission.

very own rooms, descriptions, and items. You can also get lost or confused if you jump right in." If these games sound interesting, check out the USENET newsgroups under the hierarchy *rec.games*. Read the postings and then read and study the FAQs for "your" games.

UNIX ON THE INTERNET

Once you're a regular on the Internet, you'll notice that a lot of computers out there run the UNIX operating system. UNIX was, and is, popular among researchers and computer science departments (which made up the early Internet), partly because some of the first versions of TCP/IP were distributed free with one version of UNIX known as the Berkeley Software Distribution (BSD). Many computer companies sell their machines with UNIX and TCP/IP bundled in, which makes it a more popular combination than some of the other computers and operating systems for which people have to order TCP/IP support separately.

You don't have to be a UNIX expert to use the Internet, but it doesn't hurt to know some of the basic commands. UNIX—fairly or unfairly—has gotten a reputation for being unfriendly. If you're using the Internet, however, sooner or later you'll have to deal with UNIX face-to-face, so included in this chapter is a summary of commands (see page 117).

The UNIX file system (the way files are organized on the hard disk) is hierarchical, similar to the DOS file system. If you understand how the DOS file system works, then it shouldn't take you long to find your way around UNIX systems. Since a good number of the public file archive sites are computers running the UNIX operating system, learning your way up and down a UNIX directory (as we discussed in Chapter 4) will come in pretty handy. Knowing how to navigate through directories and use some of the basic UNIX commands will make you a more powerful Internet user. See the appendix for more UNIX resources.

SECURITY ISSUES

Computer security is a major issue no matter where you go, what type of computer you use, or whether or not your computer is connected to a network. No doubt you've heard stories about breakins on the Internet and would like to know what you should be concerned about. You might be wondering, "Can people read my email, can they login to my computer? Will my computer get a virus?" This section will provide some interesting insight into security on the Internet and the answers to those questions.

First of all, you should realize that despite its military origins, the Internet is not a classified network. The AR-PANET was a network research experiment, so there was a

COMMON UNIX COMMANDS

To find out more about a command, use the *man* (for manual)
command. For example, to find out about the change
directory command, *cd*, type **man cd**.

File Commands

ls	—list files
more, page	—display file at your terminal
cp	—copy file
mv	—move or rename files
rm	—remove files

Editor

vi	—screen editor

Directory Commands

cd	—change current directory
mkdir	—make a new directory
rmdir	—remove a directory
pwd	—print working directory

Command Information

apropos	—locate commands by keyword lookup
whatis	—display command description
man	—displays manual pages online

Useful Information Commands

cal	—print calendar
date	—print date and time
who	—print who and where users are logged in

lot of collaboration with information being transferred between machines and researchers. Collaboration is difficult
if computers are locked up tight. Besides, the ARPANET was
a small community, and users left their doors unlocked, just
as trusting folks in small towns do. Today, the Internet is a
massive cooperative with thousands of networks—about
20,000 times larger than the ARPANET, all "tied" together.
And because there's still a lot of research being conducted,

it's still considered an open, "sharing" network. That doesn't mean, however, that security is not an issue. Sensitive information is stored on computers on the Internet and is therefore vulnerable to attacks from intruders. To further complicate matters, the Internet has spread its tentacles worldwide. Any computer directly connected to any network is potentially at risk if proper precautions are not taken.

What's not so secure about the Internet? Basically, the computers: different computers running different operating systems, each with its own characteristics, bugs, misconfigured software, and so forth. The security of each computer is the responsibility of a system administrator. Since all parts must work together to make the entire Internet "secure," it's probably best to assume that things aren't secure and act accordingly. If you follow a few simple rules, you'll probably be okay. Compromises in security have happened and will continue to happen. Fortunately, when they do, lessons are learned, "holes" or weaknesses get fixed, problems are highlighted, and the Internet takes another step toward becoming a bit more secure.

Breaking Down Account Doors

The press regularly reports on hackers breaking into computers and causing damage. The term "hacker" seems now to describe any denizen of the night or fourteen-year-old out on an electronic joy ride. Actually, a more accurate term for these computer hooligans is **cracker**. **Hacker** in the computer world is a term of respect: Hackers are basically nuts about computers and like to learn systems inside and out. Real hackers aren't angels, but they don't get their kicks from breaking into other systems to exploit holes and to snoop into someone else's information. Most breakins are accomplished by incredible patience and brute force. There isn't anything magical about those who do it. "Cookbook" recipes, giving step-by-step instructions on how to break into certain systems, have even been published over the network.

hacker [originally, someone who makes furniture with an axe] n. 1. A person who enjoys exploring the details of programmable systems and how to stretch their capabilities, as opposed to most users, who prefer to learn only the minimum necessary. 2. One who programs enthusiastically (even obsessively) or who enjoys programming rather than just theorizing about programming. 3. A person capable of appreciating hack value. 4. A person who is good at programming quickly. 5. An expert at a particular program, or one who frequently does work using it or on it; as in 'a UNIX hacker'. (Definitions 1 through 5 are correlated, and people who fit them congregate.) 6. An expert or enthusiast of any kind. One might be an astronomy hacker, for example. 7. One who enjoys the intellectual challenge of creatively overcoming or circumventing limitations. 8. [deprecated] A malicious meddler who tries to discover sensitive information by poking around. Hence *password hacker, network hacker*.

It is better to be described as a hacker by others than to describe oneself that way. Hackers consider themselves something of an elite (a meritocracy based on ability), though one to which new members are gladly welcome. There is thus a certain ego satisfaction to be had in identifying yourself as a hacker (but if you claim to be one and are not, you'll quickly be labeled bogus).

Source: *The New Hacker's Dictionary*, edited by Eric S. Raymond, with assistance and illustrations by Guy L. Steele Jr. (Cambridge, Mass.: The MIT Press, 1991). Reprinted with permission.

What Can You Do?

As a user of the Internet, you can't do much about fixing problems if the computer you're getting Internet access from is not your own. There is, however, something very important that you can and must do. You can stop an

Stalking the Wily Hacker

Clifford Stoll, an astronomer working as a pro-grammer at Lawrence Berkeley Labs (LBL) to make ends meet, traced a 75-cent accounting error on one of the lab's computers through the Internet until he found a German spy selling computer secrets to the KGB. Stoll documented this chase in a surprisingly exciting, can't-put-it-down book called *The Cuckoo's Egg*. *The Cuckoo's Egg* is a great introduction to the world of research networking, the Internet, and AR-PANET, and it manages to appeal to novices and experts alike.

intruder in his or her tracks simply by being responsible about the password(s) you use.

Most levels of service on the Internet require some type of authentication to prove it's really you accessing the service. Usually this involves a user identification and a password to allow access. Your userid is usually very well known, so the only way you can protect is with a secret password. Your password is the key to the locked door of your account or your electronic mail service. Most common security problems can be prevented by simply being careful with your password.

If an "undesirable" gets your password and uses it to enter your account uninvited, worse things can happen than just your files being looked at, modified, or deleted. Crackers have posted articles to newsgroups or mailing lists from an account they shouldn't be using. You may find that, without your knowledge, "you" made an insulting, politi-cally incorrect statement that infuriated everyone who read it. No matter how many followup apology messages you send to rectify the situation, damage will have been done. A lot of people may not get your real message, and many won't believe you.

Never give anyone your password. But if you do have a valid reason for giving someone your password so he can obtain some information or perform an action, change the password as soon as he's done. If you get an account on another system, such as a public database or bulletin board, do not use the same password that you use on your local system. You have no way of knowing where it is stored or how private passwords on other systems are. Don't write your password down and leave the paper in an obvious place, such as the desk drawer next to your computer. Some computers tell you upon login when you were last seen on that account. You should check to make sure it agrees with when *you* were really last logged into that computer. If there's a discrepancy, call your system administrator.

Copying the scams that try to get your credit card number over the phone, some potential intruders call or send email claiming to be a system administrator. This person will tell you that, for various reasons, you need to change the password for your account to something he tells you. Be careful of anyone claiming to be a system administrator. If you're not sure, get a number and call him back or try to see him in person.

How to Pick a Password.   An easily guessable password is one of the most common causes of security problems. If you don't know how to change your password, put it at the top of your list of things to learn. Passwords should never be based on your own name—not even your name spelled backwards. They should also not be easily guessable, such as your husband's or wife's name, girlfriend's or boyfriend's name, the dog's name, your license plate, the street where you live, your birthday—you get the picture. Passwords also should not be dictionary words. Crackers often use online dictionaries and programs to guess words by "brute force."

So what *can* passwords be? There's nothing left to pick, right? Well, be creative. Take your favorite saying, "Until the cows come home, sweetheart," and use the first letters from each word, "utcchs". (It's recommended that the word be at least six characters long.) This way the password is not a word, but it's easy to remember and hard to guess. You can also combine words, such as "car-bike." It's also recommended to mix some numbers with the letters and throw in some punctuation for pizazz, but never make your password all numbers.

Can People Read My Email?

Can they read it? Yes, they can. Now that doesn't mean that there is always someone out there reading your email. With millions of people on the Internet, our individual messages likely get lost in the crowd. But you've got to realize that once email leaves your system, it may sit on another computer hundreds or thousands of miles away, and you have no control over who has access to it. What if that computer has a liberal security policy, or is full of security holes? The best thing to do is to realize that your email is not going to be secure and to avoid transmitting sensitive material, as already recommended in Chapter 3. Even if no one reads your email while it's in transit, the recipient could forward the message on to whomever he or she pleases.

It is possible to physically "tap" networks, just like tapping telephone lines. And if someone is able to do that, he can read anything going across those wires. But all hope is not lost: There are ways to make your email more secure. One is to encrypt it before it leaves your computer. **Encrypt** means simply that it's encoded into something that no one else can read without the proper key. Upon receipt, the message must be decrypted on the recipient's machine. There are no *automatic* mechanisms available in the Internet right now to encrypt email, but if you have the necessary software on your computer, you can do it.

Viruses

Should you lose much sleep over viruses on the Internet? Well, no, and yes. Your computer can't get a virus from using electronic mail or just telneting around to other

A Catchy Title Should Appear Here

Dave Barry, noted author and nationally syndicated humor columnist for the Miami Herald, is an Internet regular—despite the fact that he's a 'Net Non-User. His column, released worldwide on the Internet through the ClariNet UPI news service (called *clari.feature.dave_barry*), has been keeping users entertained on a weekly basis for several years. Wanting to understand the erudition and sensitivity of his articles, thousands of jacked-in Dave followers formed a USENET newsgroup called *alt.fan.dave_barry*. There, fans from Waterloo to Waxahachie discuss his articles and books, recent Dave sightings, those witty post card replies to his fans, and his thriving presidential campaign (his catchword is "A Catchy Slogan Should Appear Here"). When asked what he thought of his electronic devotees, the Internet, and this book, Dave had this to say: "I think it is truly a wonderful thing that, through the Miracle of Computers, millions of people can read my column instead of leading productive lives." But humor abounds on the Internet, and even researchers and educators have been known to search out a laugh.

computers. If you're just transferring text files, then you shouldn't worry; they're not going to reach out and "grab" your computer and do something to it. You should, however, treat public domain and shareware *software* (available via anonymous FTP from public file archive sites) with caution. If you remember that you have to do a *binary* file transfer to get this software, you will be aware that you're transferring something that could possibly carry a virus. To guard against viruses from the Internet and elsewhere, you should make sure you have the best available virus-detection software installed on your computer. And keep it updated; new viruses appear all of the time.

Where there's a problem, a solution is usually near at hand, and security advice is available on the Internet. The Computer Emergency Response Team (CERT) focuses on the security needs of the research community. Based at Carnegie Mellon University, CERT has an anonymous FTP archive of security advisories, tips, tools, and so on. The computer name is *ftp.cert.org*. There's also a LISTSERV called *VIRUS-L*, a moderated, digested mail forum for discussing computer virus issues. The USENET newsgroup *comp.virus* has the same messages as *VIRUS-L*, only in a slightly different, nondigested format. The VIRUS-L FAQ document answers questions on how to get the latest free/shareware antivirus programs. It's available on the CERT public archive in the directory *pub/virus-l*, filename *FAQ.virus-l*. See the appendix for suggested reading and resources on security.

INTERNET ORGANIZATIONS

The Internet has spawned a number of organizations and interest groups over the years with many different missions and purposes. Some are special interest groups; some are task groups responsible for certain aspects of the Internet. The acronym names of these groups alone are staggering. Two organizations that may be of interest and that provide direction and information for the entire Internet are the Internet Society and the Electronic Frontier Foundation (EFF). The Internet Society deals with technical and operational issues that affect the entire Internet. The Electronic Frontier Foundation's concerns extend beyond the networks to cover all of the social and policy issues that arise as we integrate computers and networks into our culture.

The Internet Society

The Internet Society is a nonprofit professional organization run by its members (both individuals and organizations in various communities, including academic, scientific, and engineering), dedicated to encouraging cooperation among

The Electronic Frontier

"Whether by one telephonic tendril or millions, [these computers] are all connected to one another. Collectively, they form what their inhabitants call the Net. It extends across that immense region of electron states, microwaves, magnetic fields, light pulses and thought which sci-fi writer William Gibson named Cyberspace.

"Cyberspace, in its present condition, has a lot in common with the 19th Century West. It is vast, un-mapped, culturally and legally ambiguous, verbally terse (unless you happen to be a court stenographer), hard to get around in, and up for grabs. In this silent world, all conversation is typed. To enter it, one forsakes both body and place and becomes a thing of words alone. It is, of course, a perfect breeding ground for both outlaws and new ideas about liberty."

Excerpted from John Perry Barlow, "Crime and Puzzlement: Desperadoes of the DataSphere," *Whole Earth Review* (Sausalito, Calif., Fall 1990), pp. 45-57. Used with permission.

computer networks to enable a global research communications infrastructure. The society sponsors several groups that determine the needs of the Internet and propose solutions to meet them. One of these groups is the Internet Architecture Board (IAB), which provides direction to two principal task forces: the Internet Engineering Task Force (IETF) and the Internet Research Task Force (IRTF). The IETF is concerned with operational and technical issues of the Internet, and the IRTF is involved in research and development matters.

The society is also dedicated to promoting Internet technology for scientific and educational applications and to educating others in possible uses of the Internet. In addition to sponsoring a yearly international conference,

Reporting the November 1988
Internet Virus

On the morning of November 2, 1988, I received a call about a rogue program that had spun madly out of control across a remarkable number of Internet sites, temporarily disabling thousands of computers around the country. It seemed like an interesting story.

I began calling computer systems managers around the Internet, who told me that a virus or a worm had crashed naval research laboratory computers in San Diego as well as machines at Lawrence Livermore Laboratories.

Estimates of the infection's spread ranged from 60,000 to 250,000 computers attached to the Internet.

News media around the country were scrambling to get the story. *The New York Times*, however, got a key break when an unidentified caller began a series of strained conversations with me. Whoever he was, he knew a great deal about the program and how it was written. It was, the caller said, an experiment by

(Continued)

INET, it publishes a quarterly journal that provides information about the evolution of the Internet and articles of interest.

The Electronic Frontier Foundation

The EFF was founded in 1990 to "help civilize the electronic frontier; to make it truly useful and beneficial to everyone, not just an elite; and to do this in a way that is in keeping with our society's highest traditions of the free and open flow of information and communication." The catalyst for EFF's founding was the heavy-handed investigation of supposed "computer crimes" by Secret Service agents who, as

"Mr. X," a Boston-area computer scientist, that had gone awry.

My caller was himself a graduate student, a close friend of Mr. X, who was worried about the programmer's welfare. But he made a mistake. In one of our conversations he referred to Mr. X as "RTM."

For anyone who frequents computer hacker circles, RTM is immediately identifiable as a computer login. Running a command called *finger* remotely over the Internet located the login on a computer at Harvard. The person who had written the virus was Robert Tappan Morris, a 23-year-old Cornell computer science student. The bombshell, of course, was that he was the son of Robert Morris, the chief scientist of the National Computer Security Center, an arm of the N.S.A.

The Federal Bureau of Investigation conducted a wide-ranging investigation and the U.S. attorney in Syracuse recommended that the younger Mr. Morris be charged with a single misdemeanor. However, apparently the Justice Department, concerned that example be set in the case, held out for a stiffer set of charges.

Excerpted with permission from a column written by John Markoff in 1989.

the stories go, hardly knew a disk drive from a discus. In addition to practically bankrupting a couple of innocent small businesses, the investigations rode roughshod over the free speech and privacy rights of electronic communications. EFF's most famous founder, Mitch Kapor, developer of Lotus 1-2-3 and current president of ON Technology, led the charge in finding funding and hiring lawyers to assist in defense. The EFF has continued to represent computer network users in debates on public policy covering privacy, law enforcement procedures for computer crime, network development, and more.

FINDING EMAIL ADDRESSES: THE SEQUEL

We talked briefly about finding email addresses in Chapter 3. Now that you know more about using Telnet, FTP, and email, here are a few more advanced methods for tracking down email addresses. Literally millions of people can be reached via electronic mail. And, as you've seen, the Internet is growing by leaps and bounds, with more computers and people being added every hour. People are getting "on" but are having a hard time locating the people with whom they wish to communicate.

Unfortunately, there is no *one* way to find email addresses. You simply need to be an electronic detective. There isn't a central database, nor is there a distributed database directory system for you to query. If you are willing to "feel" your way around the Internet, though, you can probably find someone's email address, or at least get close. Some of the most common methods are mentioned here.

Finding an email address on a network is similar to finding telephone numbers and snail-mail addresses using the phone book or directory assistance. On the Internet, the resource is called **directory services.** More specifically, the Internet **white pages** offer the location information (such as email and telephone) similar to that provided by the telephone book's white pages. Similarly, Internet **yellow pages** are organized by type of service or by network resource.

Unfortunately, the directories now available are limited to specific organizations or groups. Providing comprehensive directory service information is difficult for several reasons. First, many people have more than one address, and those addresses can change often. For example, you may have a CompuServe address, an Internet address from a commercial Internet service, and a BITNET address from a local university. Each of these addresses has a slightly different format and is part of a different organization's directory system.

To compound matters, computer names can change; therefore, your email address may change. Privacy and security are other issues; you may wish for your CompuServe address to remain private but be willing to publicize the others. Some organizations don't wish to release their entire directories of contact information. And some others just don't have directory information compiled yet, due to lack of staff or other reasons. Committees, working groups, and standards bodies have wrestled with the directory problem, and they are working on a new directory services standard called X.500. But don't hold your breath waiting for a complete worldwide directory system any time soon.

Network Information Servers and Tools

Some well-known services and methods for finding email addresses are discussed below. Basically, you have to know a lot about people you're trying to reach in order to query a database or service to reach them. It helps if you know where they're located, what organization they work for, what university they attend, or what network provider they're getting access from. If you have that information, try to find an online directory for that group. If you want to play around and try to find the location information (electronic mail address, telephone number, and so forth) for Clifford Stoll, author of *The Cuckoo's Egg*, here are a few things to try and a few places to look.

WHOIS. (Yes, that's *who is!*) **WHOIS** is a database of information on domains, networks, hosts, and people at the Defense Data Network (DDN) Network Information Center (NIC), which is an official Internet Registry run by Government Systems, Inc. of Chantilly, Va. It is by no means an exhaustive database; it contains information on computers and users who have actually been registered (or registered themselves). WHOIS is a good place to start, though, if you have no other clue about where to begin. The DDN NIC can help you find a point of contact for many organizations, which you can use to send email to find out more information.

You can access the DDN NIC WHOIS database three ways. First, you can send electronic mail to the NIC's automatic mail service, which operates just like the info servers mentioned in Chapter 4. Basically, you send email to *service@nic.ddn.mil* and place the commands in the subject (nothing in the message body), and the response is emailed back to you. (If you want to get help information, just send the command **help** in the subject.) If you'd like to test this out, send the command **whois stoll, cliff** in the subject. This method is the only way for people to get information from the WHOIS database if they don't have direct Internet access.

If you do have direct access to the Internet, you can login remotely to the WHOIS database and use it interactively: Telnet to *nic.ddn.mil*. There's no login routine required; you just type the command **whois** and you're off and running. Make liberal use of the **help** command to learn how to use the system.

The final way to contact the DDN NIC uses the client/server method (see Chapter 4). Many computers have a **whois** client program available on their systems. If you have this available and you're on a UNIX operating system, you can type **whois -h nic.ddn.mil stoll, cliff**. The whois client is available for other systems and may require a slightly different command format. (You may not need to specify the *-h nic.ddn.mil* part.) Your client program will contact the WHOIS server on *nic.ddn.mil* and return an answer.

Other WHOIS Databases. If you have a client program running on your local system, you can contact similar databases at other organizations. Instead of the *-h nic.ddn.mil* (which sets the server host to *nic.ddn.mil*), you can substitute the name of any computer that is running a whois server.

More of these servers are being made available. Check the appendix to find out how to obtain a regularly updated list.

Finger

A program called **finger** is available on many computers directly connected to the Internet, and many people use it to find information about users on other computers. It's simple to use: Type **finger** *name@hostname*. When you use finger, you have to know what computer the user is on. You do not, however, always have to know the exact login name of the user. You can usually use any part of the person's name and finger will return essential data on all the users with that name on that computer. The type of information finger returns (depending on how much is available) includes their name, login name, office and location, phone number, and so on. Many organizations make their entire online directory available and searchable using finger. Usually these are located on "official" or well-known computers. You can also use finger to find out about all the users logged into a computer at any one time. To do this locally, just type **finger**. Or to check for all the users at a remote system, you can type **finger**@*remote-host-name*. Unfortunately, finger isn't available on all computers, or it may be disabled for security reasons, so you can't depend on it to provide all the answers. One of the more obvious security reasons is because many people don't want others to know where they are or when they were on the computer last.

Some organizations use finger to provide often-updated information, such as the weather or daily headlines. These include NASA Daily News, which you can get by issuing the command **finger nasanews@space.mit.edu**, and up-to-date earthquake reports by issuing the command **finger quake@geophys.washington.edu**.

Other Methods

Here are some other ideas for finding email addresses. If

your friend is at a university, you might check to see if there is a CWIS (Campus Wide Information System) that can help you locate her electronically. USENET has an address database of all the people who have posted articles to USENET, which has proved very useful. To use this service, send email to *mail-server@pit-manager.mit.edu* and put the command **send usenet-addresses**/*name* in the subject or body of the message; *name* should be the various name or names you're looking for. The service offers a very "liberal" search method—for example, you could search on the name "aQuey" and it will return an address for Tracy LaQuey. In other words, you can include part of a name and the service will return all occurrences of it. This USENET database is also searchable via WAIS (Wide Area Information Servers); the WAIS database is called *usenet-addresses*.

Interfaces to Multiple Databases and Servers.   Some popular services provide information on multiple organizations or directory services. These services access multiple directory servers. Here's some information on how to access them.

PSI's White Pages Service (a well-known X.500 pilot project) provides access to directory information for more than 75 organizations. You can test it out by remotely logging in using telnet to *wp.psi.com*, login **fred**.

Knowbot Information Service (KIS) is based on the concept of a **knowbot**—a knowledge robot that knows how to navigate networks in search of information. KIS queries a number of directory services to help you find directory assistance information. You can remotely login to this service at: *nri.reston.va.us 185*. Or send email to *netaddress@nri.reston.va.us*. Include the command **help** in the body of the message.

Netfind is similar to the Knowbot Information Service in that it provides a "one-stop shop" service that knows which directory services, databases, or computers to contact, based on the keywords (login name, first and last name, organization) that you supply. However, Netfind is more thorough and uses more widespread methods than KIS to find information. You can query Netfind by remotely logging into *bruno.cs.colorado.edu*, login **netfind**.

Directory Assistance for Computers.   On occasion, you will need to get a computer's IP address. (Perhaps the host name you've been using just doesn't work anymore.) The necessary tools may or may not be available on your system. If they're not, check to see if an alternative tool is offered. Two well-known tools are *nslookup* and *dig*. To use either, just invoke them with the name of the computer. For example, **nslookup nic.ddn.mil** will return the IP address: 192.112.36.5, or the command **dig nnsc.nsf.net** will return 128.89.1.178. (Unless those numbers have changed, which is entirely possible!)

HELP! GETTING MORE INFORMATION

As it was so well put in the FAQ on MUDS, "What if I'm completely confused and am casting about for a rope in a vast, churning wilderness of chaos and utter incomprehension?" If you're confused and have questions and don't know where to turn, here are a few survival tips. First of all, realize that you're not alone and that we all started off feeling dazed and bewildered. Everyone's digital digestive system is different; sometimes it takes a while to get the drift of all of this. Remember, even *net.veterans* don't know all of this!

Once you know you have a problem, the biggest hurdle is finding out what exactly it is! The kinds of things that stump people include figuring out what they can do from their system (what applications they can use, what levels of services are available to them); how to use the applications; how to diagnose problems once they do figure out the applications; and, after they've learned those ropes, finding the resources that will help them.

Where to Start

Start close to home when you look for help. Consultants

who understand the applications running on your system or network will be able to give you the best assistance. Be as specific as possible when you do ask for help. Write down error messages exactly (including all numbers and punctuation) as you see them on the screen and try to recall the chain of events that got you into trouble.

If you're getting network access through work or college, there may be a local consulting office or helpdesk that can give you information about available services, such as documentation, manuals, and online help. Some helpdesks are starting to offer their own online Gopher systems that provide easy-to-use interfaces to steer you in the right direction, help you to learn about your local network and the Internet, and provide links into other systems.

If you are getting (or planning to get) your Internet access through a commercial provider, you'll need to look to them for information and services. Ask about support before you sign up. (Chapter 6 provides information about the types of connections and applications that are available.) Commercial providers have telephone hotlines for support, provide documentation about their services, and have an email address to write for more information.

Other Sources of Help

Network Information Centers.   NICs offer information about the Internet and their networks and services. Your network isn't required to have a NIC, but if it does, check out what they have to offer. NICs are springing up around the Internet; all the nationwide backbones have them, as well as most of the midlevel and regional networks. These organizations vary in size and services; many provide online guides, newsletters, and tutorials. Others offer seminars and classes. This may be more information than you'll ever need, but it's useful to familiarize yourself with what's available.

As the Internet continues to grow and evolve into the NREN, user and information services will become a more important part of network operation. The NSF recently requested proposals for new national information services (NIS). These services would include registration, directory, database, and information on Internet education. The groups were not yet named as this book went to press.

The NSF Network Service Center.   The NNSC provides help and services in general for the NSFNET. You can check out its online information via anonymous FTP on the host *nnsc.nsf.net*. One of the more interesting items for new users is an *Internet Tour* Hypercard stack, which includes information about the history of the Internet as well as tutorial sessions on electronic mail, FTP, and Telnet. That's in the *internet-tour* directory. For instructions on getting and installing it, get the *Internet-Tour-README* file.

The NNSC also maintains an online *Internet Resource Guide*, organized into seven categories: Computational Resources, Library Catalogs, Archives, White Pages, Networks, Network Information Centers, and Miscellaneous Resources. You can get the guide on the *nnsc.nsf.net* host (available via anonymous FTP) in the *resource-guide* directory. Get the *README* file in that directory for information about how to get and use the guide.

The Defense Data Network (DDN) Network Information Center.   This NIC has often been referred to as *The* NIC. If you're considering connecting your organization's network to the Internet, these are the people to talk to. (If you're getting organizational access via a commercial Internet provider, however, you may not have to contact the DDN NIC). The DDN NIC acts as the U.S. Internet Registrar for domains and network numbers, maintains the WHOIS database, provides an online repository of information available for anonymous FTP from *nic.ddn.mil*. The information is also available by sending an email message to *service@nic.ddn.mil*. To get information on how to use this mail-server, send email to that address with the command **help** in the subject, nothing in the message body.

The SRI Network Information Systems Center.   SRI offers the *Internet Information Series* documents, including *Internet: Getting Started.* This very useful book explains the Internet in detail and also provides good information for organizations wishing to connect. The NISC offers as well archives of mailing lists and technical documents on CD ROM called *The TCP/IP CD,* and it has an anonymous FTP archive of useful information on host *ftp.nisc.sri.com.*

Helpful Online Information

Once you're on the network, you may hear about RFCs (requests for comments). RFCs are documents that detail protocol standards, procedures, general information, and sometimes even lighthearted poems and April Fool jokes about the Internet. Unless you 're interested in knowing the nitty gritty, bit-level details about TCP/IP, you probably won't want to look at these RFCs.

There is, however, a series of RFCs called *For Your Information* documents (FYIs). FYIs are introductory in nature, explaining Internet concepts rather than detailing protocol specifications. Many of these documents were compiled and written by members of the User Services Working Group, one of the working groups in the Internet Engineering Task Force mentioned earlier in this chapter, charged with providing introductory information and general help for new Internet users. FYIs are available from a number of places, including the DDN NIC (anonymous FTP to host *nic.ddn.mil,* **cd** to the **rfc** directory). Get the file *fyi-index.txt* for a list of available documents. You can also send electronic mail to *rfc-info@isi.edu* and, in the body of the message, put the command **help: ways_to_get_rfcs**. A help message will be returned to you.

You may feel as though you've earned an Internet advanced degree by now. But, unless you already have access through your work or college, you're probably just itching to get connected to the Internet. Our last chapter deals with the nitty-gritty of getting on the Internet: finding the right modem and software, deciding what kind of access *you* need, and locating commercial or alternative Internet access. Stay with us: You're almost at home on the Internet!

Chapter 6

GETTING CONNECTED

*N*ow that you know what you want to do on the Internet, or at least where you want to go exploring, you'll want to get connected. There isn't just one place you can go to get access to the Internet; as we have said, paths to the Internet are many. The best one for you will depend on your circumstances, your needs, and—to some extent—your pocketbook. This chapter tells you what you need to get started, your choices for individual access and where to go for services, and the basics for connecting a business organization.

If you work for an institution or a company with full-time access through a network connection to the Internet, you have the shortest path of all. All you need to do is sit down at your office terminal or workstation and, using the instructions supplied by your in-house computer gurus, log on and get going. Most Internet connections have been made just like that—as connections between two networks, rather than two computers. For example, a college's local area network (LAN) would get access to the Internet by making a connection through a leased phone line to a regional network. Once that connection is made, in most cases every computer on the local area network has "full-time" access, with Internet access available all the time, day and night.

ALL YOU NEED TO GET STARTED

Fortunately, there are less involved and less expensive ways to get access to the Internet if you're an individual computer user or small business. All you need is a personal computer (Mac, PC, whatever), a modem, communications software, and a phone line. Connecting an entire business or organization's network is more complex than we can cover in detail, but we've included an overview of the basics later in this chapter in the section, "Connecting Your Business or Organization." Some sources for more information are given, as well.

Modems

Modems are, simply put, computer appliances that convert the digital signal from your computer into an analog sound wave that can be transmitted over telephone lines. A modem at the other end converts the analog signal back to a digital signal that can be read by the computer you're talking to. Exciting advances are being made in modem technology, with faster speeds and more error-free data transmission. High-speed modems can reduce errors from line noise and even do data compression. As with any computer-related purchase, you should buy the very best modem you can afford—perhaps even a bit better than you can afford. Technology changes fast, and five years from now, today's high-speed modems will be as obsolete as that dinosaur of modems, the 300 bps acoustic coupler.

The ideal modem for telecommunications communicates at high speeds and has error correction and data compression features. Error correction protocols help filter out line noise, which throws "garbage" characters like {{pdf{{{ on your screen, and they ensure an error-free transmission. Data compression, while a useful feature, may not help you much on some bulletin boards and information services that have already compressed their files, in which case *your* modem can't compress them any further. Shopping for a modem gets you into a complexity of feature combinations: speed, modulation protocols, data compression, and more. Claims, particularly for speed, may not be what they appear to be. So it could be wise, especially if you are planning to spend a lot for a high-speed modem, to check some independent sources before you buy.

Most people (getting individual access) are still using 2400 bps modems to access the Internet and for other services. They may not be lightning fast, but 2400 bps modems are inexpensive, easily available, and nothing to be embarrassed about. All of the access and information systems support them, and, for the occasional user, the difference in online and/or long-distance charges (the higher your modem speed, of course, the less time it takes you to get information) will not be too significant. If you plan to spend a lot of time online, however, or need quick, error-free access, spring for a high-speed modem with error correction and data compression.

Communications Software

Communications software, which is installed on your computer, sets up the three-way conversation between your computer, the modem, and the remote computer. Some modems come bundled with communications software. If yours isn't, try to buy them together from a knowledgeable dealer so that you'll have minimal frustration in getting everything to work.

Almost all 2400 bps modems are Hayes-compatible and will work seamlessly with virtually every communications software package on the market for the PC or the Mac. They are easy to install and set up. Some of the features you'll want to look for in a communications package are a full range of file transfer protocols (that is, Xmodem, Ymodem, Zmodem, Kermit, and others, which are different from the Internet's FTP) and terminal emulations such as VT-100 and VT-102. Once you enter the world of high-speed modems, though, it is not so simple.

Your communications software must support **terminal**

emulation, which means that your computer essentially becomes a terminal on the computer you're connected to. The VT-100 terminal emulation is probably the most used and most supported of all the terminal emulations. The VT-100 was a venerable terminal produced in the millions by Digital Equipment Corporation (DEC). Its keyboard layout and interface have become a standard for computer-to-computer communications over the years.

Finding Phone Access

Finding an economical way to dial in to your chosen system is a big concern. Long-distance telephone and access charges can easily exceed your costs for connect time on the computer. Every provider offers a local (to them) number for direct dial-up; some provide local numbers in major cities or in areas they consider to be their prime territory. If your chosen system is an expensive long-distance call away, you can check out some of the public data networks and dialup services below that make a business of providing computer/phone connections. Many of these services provide for online or phone signup and accept major credit cards.

CompuServe Packet Network (CPN).   CompuServe has hundreds of local-access phone numbers all over the United States and Canada. You need not subscribe to CompuServe's information service to use CPN—you'll be billed for your use through your provider. If your chosen system allows CPN access, dial CompuServe's information service, (800) 848-4480, to find your closest CPN access number. Hit <RETURN> to get to the HOST NAME: prompt and enter the command **phones** to use their number lookup service.

PC Pursuit.   PC Pursuit is a U.S. Sprint service that provides flat rate, off-hours dialup services to cities all over the United States. Users pay a one-time registration fee and a monthly fee that covers 30 hours of non-prime-time use. Excess hours are billed at a low hourly rate. Call (800)

736-1130 to set up an account or to get more information. In order to sign up online, use your modem and dial 1-(800)-877-2006.

Three Other Services. TAC Access from UUNET Technologies, PSI's Global Dialing Service, and CERFnet's Dial n' CERF's 800 services can give you local or 800 service Internet access. (These services are explained later in this chapter.)

TYPES OF INDIVIDUAL CONNECTIONS

You have your modem set up and your software installed; you've even read the manuals and practiced a little. Perhaps you're a veteran telecommunicator and just want to get right to the Internet. Depending on the kind of connection you are using, individuals can have *access* to the Internet or a direct Internet *connection*. Whichever you have, you will be "dialing into" the Internet. Following are some of your connection options.

Dialup Terminal Emulation

What It Is. Using the terminal emulation feature in your communications software, your computer essentially becomes a terminal on a remote computer system. You can get access to the Internet by dialing "into" a computer that has a full-time Internet connection. If you have communications software that does terminal emulation, such as Kermit, Procomm, or Whiteknight, then all you need is an account on an Internet-connected computer.

Having an account means that you are allowed to login with a userid and password and use the services and disk space of that computer. By dialing into an Internet-connected computer, you will have access to all the basic services on the Internet—that is, remote login, file transfer, and electronic mail. Many computers that allow this kind of access run the UNIX operating system, so you may need

Serious Games

Parallelling world events such as the 1990 Gulf War, university-sponsored computer simulations play out real-world political dramas on the Internet stage. In early 1990 these computer simulations started in the Middle East Politics classes at Melbourne University in Australia, connected with foreign relations classes at the University of Texas and Macquarie University, Australia.

Students were divided into teams of 1 to 5 people each (simulations generally have 40 to 150 teams), and each team assumed the role of a political leader in the Middle East or in another vitally interested country such as the United States, the United Kingdom, or France. One team played Yasser Arafat, while others played President Bush, the Prime Minister of Israel, and the King of Saudi Arabia. The teams extensively researched their characters to help them play the assigned roles in realistic fashion.

The controllers (usually the class lecturers) then set an initial scenario (typically the assassination of a prominent figure, an invasion, or whatever seemed like fun) and the various teams responded, using email (and "talk" where possible) to communicate with each other. Each team tried to advance its own goals and strategies, almost always at the expense of someone else.

The amount of mail flying back and forth was tremendous. Over the three-week simulation period, most teams received about 1,500 to 2,000 messages. Many general "press release" type of missives went out to all players, supplemented by roughly 200 to 250 personal messages for each team. Aside from the mail, lots of the wheeling and dealing took place over "talk" as well.

(Continued)

In a sense the Internet became the stage on which these games of global diplomacy were played out. In the past, such simulations used letters which "runners" carried back and forth. Using email and the Internet improves the concept tremendously. Most of the standard advantages of email apply, including speed, imperviousness to distance, and the ability to log in from almost anywhere, rather than being confined to one specific location.

During the 1990 Mideast computer simulation, the participants managed to *talk* Saddam Hussein into leaving Kuwait without going to war. Otherwise, events in the simulations tended to mirror real life to an astonishing degree. At one point, one of the "characters" was killed off in a simulation, only to have his real-life counterpart die a few weeks later. Players threaten, cajole, bribe, fall in love, blackmail, and occasionally shoot at each other. A lot of hot air is vented, and things generally don't change very much in the end, which is pretty much the way the Middle East is in reality.

The concept's popularity is growing; other simulations occurred in 1991, and probably are going on right now as you read this, holding the mirror up to nature and playing out alternate scripts to reality on the Internet.

Source: Joseph D'Cruz, Research Assistant at Melbourne University, Australia.

to be familiar with some of the UNIX commands mentioned in Chapter 5.

Who Does It?   Public Access systems (see below), including CERFnet, The World, MSEN, and NETCOM, offer dialup terminal emulation. With a little detective work, you may find a local user group or university that offers terminal access to the Internet.

With terminal emulation, your personal computer becomes a terminal on an Internet computer.

Terminal Servers

What It Is.   Individual users can also dial into a **terminal server** instead of a computer directly on the Internet. A terminal server is basically a computer that accepts connections and allows you to use the Internet to remotely login to other computers. Terminal servers are "bouncing off" points to the Internet.

Terminal servers have modems attached to them so that users can dial in and, from there, remotely login to any computer on the Internet. Once you've dialed into a terminal server, your scope is a bit limited because, even though in most cases you have to login using a userid and password, you don't have any disk space. If you're on a trip and have access to a local terminal server, you can connect to your mainframe or workstation computer back at the office via the Internet. However, if you don't have an account on an Internet-connected computer, this service won't do you much good, unless you are content to connect to online library catalogs or information retrieval servers that allow access without a personal userid.

Keep in mind that when you dial into an Internet-connected computer or a terminal server, you can access Internet applications. The actions you perform, however, are from the standpoint of that computer, not your PC or Mac (which is just acting as a terminal) at home. If you transfer a file using FTP from a public transfer site, you're transferring it to the Internet-connected computer, *not* to your home PC or Mac. If you want that file on your home computer, you will have to transfer it again, this time from the Internet computer to your computer (using your communications software file transfer protocols, Kermit, Zmodem, and so forth). This two-step process can be cumbersome and confusing to new users.

Who Does It?   UUNet's TAC Access, CERFnet's Dial n' CERF 800 service, and PSI's Global Dialing Service (GDS) offer terminal server access.

Client Software Access

What It Is.   Client software access brings some of the Internet functions, such as electronic mail, USENET News, and file transfer, straight to your computer. Providers or services supply you with special software, known as **client** or **agent software**. With their proprietary or public domain software on your computer, you dial into your service's local access point. In addition to taking care of the communications, it also provides an email reader and an editor for composing messages.

Although you're not *interactively* using the Internet, you can download electronic mail and news and then read messages and postings at your leisure on your home computer, rather than tying up a phone line or running up connection charges. But not all the Internet's applications, particularly remote login, are available to you. These client connections, though, can be far more user-friendly than the public access systems. You work with a familiar graphic application on your PC or Macintosh, not on a foreign computer account. You also don't have to worry about taking the extra step of transferring files from the Internet computer to your home computer (as you do with dialup terminal emulation access); the software does all of this for you.

Who Does It?   InterCon's Worldlink is a good example of a client connection, as is PSI's PSILink. Universities also offer access using many public domain software packages (Eudora, NuPOP, Trumpet, and others).

Full-Access Dialup Connection

What It Is.   A more advanced client connection uses client networking software and a high-speed modem to actually *become* a computer on the Internet. Protocols such as Serial Line Internet Protocol (SLIP) and Point-to-Point-Protocol (PPP) bring the power and flexibility of the Internet straight to your home computer over an ordinary telephone line. SLIP and PPP are actually two different protocols that make your computer a *peer* computer on the Internet. A SLIP or PPP connection is a great way to connect, but it can be more expensive and a bit more difficult to configure. Connect charges are high in comparison with other options, and the connections usually require a fairly sophisticated high-speed modem.

When you use a SLIP/PPP connection, you are actually using file transfer and remote login on your *own* computer, not on an Internet-connected computer that you've dialed into. For example, if you want to transfer a file using FTP from a public access site, you are transferring that file straight to your home computer.

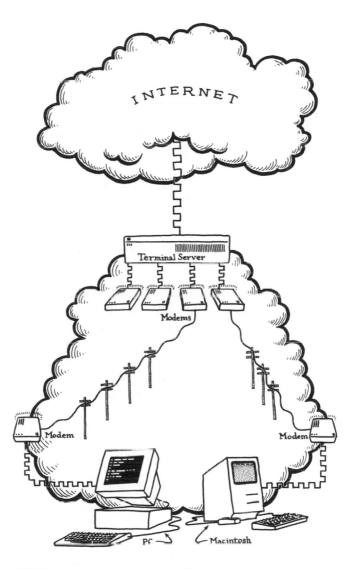

With SLIP or PPP, your computer *becomes* a host on the Internet.

You must dial into another computer or terminal server that is running SLIP (if your computer is running SLIP) or PPP (if your computer is running PPP) to make this connection. You'll also need an Internet Protocol (IP) address, because your computer needs to be identified on the network. Your IP address may stay the same or it may change every time you connect. Your provider will most likely assign you an address, or the computer or terminal server will assign you a number to use when you make the connection. You may want a registered host name as well, but as with the IP address, your network provider will probably be able to assist you.

Who Does It?   CERFnet, PSI, and many of the public access systems offer SLIP/PPP services to individual and organization systems.

CHOOSING AN INDIVIDUAL ACCESS PROVIDER

Network access for individuals is a new and evolving market, and one likely to grow very quickly. So finding the services you want, the access, and the right price is not as simple as picking a long-distance phone carrier. Internet access is offered by private companies, by universities, by academic/research networks, and by public-private partnerships. Service packages vary a great deal and change constantly, as do rates. Your options are not limited to what is in this chapter. Use the information here and in the appendix as a general guide to starting your own research.

Public Access Systems

Several companies offer dial-in access to their systems, giving you terminal emulation or (if available) SLIP/PPP access to the Internet. All of these services offer file transfer and remote login on the Internet, in addition to electronic mail and (depending on the system) a variety of other services, including commercial databases. Access is usually via a phone call to the system's local number, although some systems also offer access via public data networks such as CompuServe Packet Network (CPN). If you have access to an Internet terminal server (through a provider such as PSI), you can remotely login to these systems.

Many public access providers are expanding and adding access points in more cities, so you may want to contact them for the latest access and service information. Many of these providers offer assistance with buying and installing modems and communications software. Pricing structures vary widely, with monthly access fees, connect charges, or a combination. The services all provide for a wide range of modem speeds. See the appendix for a list of Public Access Systems.

National Providers

As mentioned in Chapter 2, there are commercial Internet providers that provide access to their own national networks and to the academic and research portion of the Internet. These providers, including CERFnet, UUNET, ANS CO+RE, Sprint, and PSI offer a wide range of access for individuals, from terminal emulation to full-time SLIP or PPP access. The appendix has a list of national providers and what each offers.

Special Interest Groups

You may be eligible for inexpensive Internet access through a special interest or professional group. Librarians and educators, for example, have led the way in providing Internet access in member groups. Who knows? A group you belong to might be offering a low-cost Internet connection. Check around.

The Cooperative Library Agency for Systems and Services (CLASS) is an excellent example of an organization offering Internet connectivity to its members. CLASS is made up of about 800 academic/public and special libraries nationwide. Because Internet access has become so popular among librarians, CLASS began providing Internet access to their members through a terminal emulation dialup 800 number to a UNIX computer system. There is a cost for an

TeleOlympics

Kids around the world caught the Olympic spirit last year as they participated in their own worldwide, "virtual" Olympics. The Academy One TeleOlympics, organized by NPTN (National Public Telecomputing Network), had more than 12,000 kids from 9 countries competing in track and field events in their own schoolyards. All of the events were held on the same day, after an opening ceremony that included a real-time chat hosted by the Cleveland FreeNet and an exchange of email among all the participating schools. Events included 50-, 400-, 800-, and 1600-meter runs (for different age groups), a long jump, and a tennis ball throw. Results were posted to the network, and medalists in each event and age category shared an electronic victory platform. The teachers made the most of the accompanying educational opportunities, and the kids had fun!

Source: Linda Delzeit, Cleveland FreeNet.

organization's first account, then extra cost for each additional account. There is also an online hourly charge. Through this system, CLASS members have access to remote login, file transfer, USENET news, and email.

More and more teachers are using computer networking in the classroom and for their own education and curriculum development. Several states offer very low-cost access to K–12 educators. If you are a teacher and are interested in finding out more about access to the Internet, then contact your district's computer coordinator or regional computing consortium to find out about your access options.

The Institute for Global Communications (IGC) was mentioned in Chapter 1 as providing access to its network and the Internet for environmental and political activists.

IGC provides an offline email reader called Global Link, similar to the client email programs described above. Check the appendix for contact information. The community FreeNets mentioned in Chapter 4 also offer access, usually to anyone who fills out an application. The appendix provides contact information for the National Public Telecomputing Network.

Electronic Mail and News Services

The wonder of the Internet is its many connecting points. If the providers we've mentioned don't suit you, an outernet (or indirect) connection may. Some of the so-called indirect (email and news only) access paths are mentioned below; to discover other available options, just ask around. Keep in mind that new services, new software, and new technology are being made available almost on a daily basis, creating new opportunities to connect directly or indirectly to the Internet.

Email Access Through Commercial Networks. If electronic mail is all you need, you have plenty of choices for an Internet connection. Most commercial online services, such as CompuServe, American Online, and MCIMail, have an electronic mail gateway to the Internet. (At this time, Prodigy does not, nor does it plan to, offer an email gateway to the Internet. This is a Frequently Asked Question!) If you have an account on one of these systems, you can send and receive email to and from anyone on the Internet. Note, however, that these services may have a per-message charge for both inbound and outbound Internet email. These charges can add up, so be sure to shop around for the best deal.

Wireless Email. Some services allow email to be forwarded from the Internet to alphanumeric pagers and portable computers equipped with radio modems. For example, RadioMail is a gateway service from Anterior Technology that provides two-way email between RadioMail subscribers and the Internet (and other commercial networks) and one-way delivery of email (from the Internet and other networks) to pagers. The two-way RadioMail service provides a transparent (to the user) connection between the worldwide wide-area land-based networks and wide-area wireless networks. For people who can't be (or don't want to be) tied to their office or home computer, RadioMail and similar services have a real advantage. It's also useful for mobile Internet users who travel frequently. See the appendix for contact information.

Email Access Through the UUCP Worldwide Network.
UUCP stands for UNIX-to-UNIX Copy Program. Basically, it is used as a method for computers to talk to each other over phone lines. Versions of UUCP are available for VMS and DOS operating systems, as well as UNIX computers.

UUCP provides for file transfer between machines. The files that are transferred often contain commands to be executed on a remote system, including printing on a remote computer or sending email. The UUCP network consists of thousands of computers all over the world that have agreed to communicate with each other via the phone lines. Because of these agreements, it is possible to send email from one computer to another by specifying exactly which computers the email must travel through to get to its destination. This process is known as "source routing." Many UUCP nodes are starting to register in the Internet domain name system (by using MX records), so they look like they're directly connected to the Internet (when, in fact, they have an agreement with an Internet-connected computer to act as a "post office," transferring email back and forth).

Although no central authority controls the UUCP network, there is a public registry that maintains information about computers whose administrators have volunteered (or remembered) to submit information. There are many email gateways between the UUCP network and the

Internet, so it is easy to send and receive email back and forth. USENET news runs over the UUCP network, so that may also be available. However, UUCP does not allow for remote login or interactive file transfer.

Going the UUCP route is usually much less expensive than other kinds of access, but it may require more research and upfront work. The equipment is simple: just your PC or Mac, modem, and phone line. The software is usually free or very inexpensive. Your expenses may include some long-distance charges. The hard part may be finding someone to agree to "connect" you, either letting you dial them up for information or having them dial you up, or both. If you ask, you may find someone in a local computer user group who'll agree to let you send information back and forth from/to their computer.

Although some universities may offer similar services, user support and reliability is not guaranteed because people are usually connecting you out of the kindness of their hearts. If you don't want to struggle to find someone or to get help, or to spend time debugging problems, you should go with a commercial UUCP email provider, where hand-holding and ongoing support are available. Those providers that offer UUCP mail and USENET news include UUNET, PSI, Anterior Technology, and many of the public access systems.

Bulletin Board Systems.   Many local bulletin board systems also provide some type of mail access to the Internet. Through these systems, you may be able to exchange UUCP or Fidonet mail and USENET news, or you may be able to dialup the system (using terminal emulation) and access mail and news interactively on the BBS system.

Find these systems by asking local computer gurus at user group meetings or by consulting the NIXPUB list, which currently lists about 127 systems and their services worldwide. NIXPUB is an access list that's maintained by a volunteer and made available via anonymous FTP and dialup UUCP. See the appendix for instructions on getting the NIXPUB list. (If you don't have direct Internet access, you may have to ask someone with Internet access to retrieve it for you.)

CONNECTING YOUR BUSINESS OR ORGANIZATION

As we said earlier, traditionally, networks are connected to the Internet, rather than single computers. These networks can be local area networks (LANs) or wide area networks (WANs), or something in between. Connecting your organization's local or wide area network to the Internet is entirely different from getting an individual connection, and it is much more involved. Space prevents us from giving much detail about what you need to do, but we'll outline some of the steps to be taken, some documentation that is available, and who you can contact for more information.

You must make your connection to the Internet through a network provider. The members of the Commercial Internet Exchange (CIX) have already been mentioned (CERFnet, PSI, US Sprint, and UUNET). Another commercial provider, Advanced Network & Services, Inc. (ANS), also offers commercial access. There are many other providers, most of which are academic and research in nature. As noted in Chapter 2, an acceptable use policy puts limits on commercial information traversing the National Science Foundation Network.

If your organization plans on using the Internet for noncommercial purposes, there is probably no problem in getting a connection through one of these mid-level networks. If, however, you would like more flexibility and you aren't sure if you can abide by any acceptable use policies, then you'll definitely want to connect to a commercial provider. That way, you're free to send any type of information to anyone as long as they are on one of these commercial networks. Additionally, all commercial providers have connections to the NSFNET, and most have agreements with each other to pass traffic back and forth.

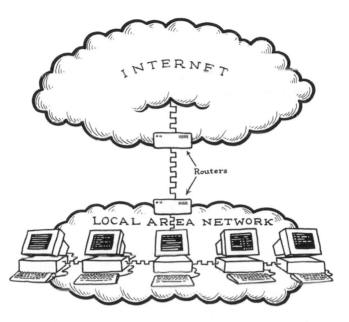

Your business or organization can connect its local area network to the Internet.

Administrative Details

Before you can make a connection, you must take care of a few administrative details—namely, registering for unique information that will identify your organization and its network to the rest of the Internet. You will need your own Internet Protocol network number (for example, 129.126) and a domain name (for example, *kodak.com*). The IP network number will be one of several classes, depending on how big your network is in terms of number of attached computers.

Once you obtain this number, you can assign separate, unique IP addresses to each computer on your network. Similarly, with a domain name you can uniquely identify your organization and each of your computers by giving them a logical name within that domain. You can obtain these key identifiers from the U.S. Internet Registrar, the

Geeks in Paradise

The Internet Engineering Task Force (IETF) is a voluntary group of network designers, engineers, vendors, and researchers who manage the protocol development and operation of the Internet. The group meets three times a year for a week of technical discussions, presentations, and problem-solving sessions. Meetings in the early years were usually near a campus network where members could remotely connect to their home computers and read their email.

As more and more people started attending the IETF meetings, it was difficult to accommodate everyone wanting to read their email from home, so the meeting hosts began providing terminal rooms. The terminal rooms started out small, usually just a bunch of terminals attached to terminal servers with a connection to the Internet through the campus or organization networks. As the Internet blossomed, however, membership did too, and soon there were so many members that the usual university meeting areas were too small to accommodate them. When the

(Continued)

Defense Data Network (DDN) Network Information Center (NIC), operated by Government Systems, Inc. You will need to complete several registration forms to apply for your IP number and domain name and send them in to the DDN NIC. These registration forms ask for certain information about your network, such as how many computers are connected to it, as well as administrative and technical contact information. If you have problems answering any of the questions on these registration forms, ask your network provider or the DDN NIC for assistance.

You'll also need to provide the names of two computers that will act as domain nameservers for host information on your network. You will recall from Chapter 2 that a domain

meetings moved to hotels, the terminal rooms became more and more elaborate. IETF members could conveniently access their work at the home office between sessions—and their coworkers didn't even know they were gone!

But things got a little out of hand at a recent IETF meeting in San Diego. Remember, these are the folks who essentially operate the Internet! The people hosting the meeting had outdone themselves this time, with the latest in workstation and networking technology, all linked together and connected to CERFnet via a T1 (1.544 Mbps) leased-line connection. This setup was in one of the hotel's meeting rooms, which had a sliding glass door and view of the Pacific. There was so much equipment that a guard was posted all night to make sure nothing was stolen. Even this Geek Mecca, however, wasn't enough for some of the network specialists, who were seen stringing and attaching cable (connected to the LAN in the terminal room) with a staple gun up the side of the hotel building so that they could bring the power of the Internet to their state-of-the-art laptops in the privacy of their own rooms. That hotel was wired!

nameserver is a computer that has a database of information about the computers on your network. (The type of information in this database includes each computer's name, Internet address, and computer type.) Two servers are required for reliability purposes, one designated primary, the other secondary. (Your organization can have more than one secondary nameserver.)

If one server (perhaps the primary one) is unavailable (perhaps for hardware reasons or because the network is down), the other will be able to answer queries for computer addresses and names. For this reason, it is recommended that one of these nameservers be located at some place other than your own network. Some network providers offer name service as part of their services or will act as a domain "dating service" for you, helping you to find an off-site secondary server.

Software and Equipment Needed to Connect

Because you're connecting to the Internet, you'll need to be "running" the TCP/IP protocols on the computers on your network to take full advantage of Internet applications. If you're not using TCP/IP, then you'll need to have software and equipment that knows how to translate between the Internet and your network protocols.

In order to connect your network, you will need some special equipment. This equipment will be owned, maintained, and configured by your organization or your network provider, or a combination of both. A key piece of equipment is a router, a special computer that connects to your network and also has a connection to your Internet service provider (see Chapter 2). The router takes care of forwarding packets to the proper destination. You will also need equipment known as a CSU/DSU to handle the connections between the leased lines (mentioned below) and the routers.

Connection Alternatives

There are many ways to actually make a connection to the Internet. (Surprisingly, many people think that satellites are used a lot!) Most connections are actually just leased digital data lines dedicated to telecommunication, available from telephone companies. Other possible methods (in addition to satellite) are microwave and fiber optic cables. You can also connect your organization's network through the public telephone network using the SLIP or PPP protocols described earlier in this chapter. This "on demand dialup" connection can be a lower-cost (albeit lower-performance) alternative for small organizations. Realize, however, that if you have a dialup connection, anytime you communicate the dialup connection will have to be established before

Internet to the Rescue!

Tired of those busy signals when you're trying to reach technical support for your computer? One high-tech company gets much of its hardware and software technical support over the Internet. Over the past year, they've gotten bug fixes and patches for their SUN Microsystems workstations and technical support from their router vendor, Cisco Systems. Another hardware vendor uses the Internet to login to their system for problem diagnosis and resolution.

One of the company's software engineers told us about how the Internet recently saved the day (and night) for him when his boss needed a network monitoring problem fixed by Friday morning! (and it was 4:59 PM on Thursday). A quick search into the Internet produced a gold mine of network monitoring programs. He chose one of the simpler ones, customized it, and within an hour was done and on his way home. "Another victory for Truth, Connectedness, and the Internet Way!"

Source: Peter Ho.

you're actually online. The speed of your connection can be from 9.6 kbps to 45 Mbps (commonly known as T3). It's good to know how much you plan on using the Internet when deciding on the speed of your connection.

Costs

Costs of connecting your organization's network can vary widely (or wildly) from provider to provider. Obviously, providers who do much of the work for you will charge more in administrative and monthly or yearly fees. Startup expenses include special equipment and administrative fees. After your network is connected, recurring costs include monthly administrative fees or subscriptions and leased-line charges. However, the information traffic on your leased-line links isn't metered—you won't get a long-distance bill for every file transfer an employee or student made from a computer in Brazil or every email message sent to someone in Alaska.

Other Connection Issues

Once you're connected, there are several issues that you may have to address constantly. One is technical support. If your network provider doesn't monitor, configure, and upgrade your network's connection, then you will have to pay someone to do it. Someone has to maintain the domain nameservers and establish an electronic mail system for your organization. Additionally, there can be quite a bit of user support required once you have a connection to the Internet. Many helpful people, mailing lists, and documentation are available on the Internet, but initially you may need some handholding for your users. Your network provider may assist in this, as well.

Finally, you or your network provider will be responsible for maintaining security on your network and computers. Security includes making sure you know (by using proper authorization mechanisms such as accounts and passwords on computers and terminal servers) which users on your network are accessing the Internet and keeping intruders out of your systems.

Providers

Most of the NSFNET mid-level networks are a good source for connections. There are too many to list in this book, but you can get a list and access information from one of the national NICs mentioned in Chapter 5. Commercial providers offering organizational connections include UUNET, CERFnet, US Sprint, ANS, and PSI. See the listings in the appendix.

A very informative book, *Internet: Getting Started,* published by SRI International, contains lists of providers organized by region. Updated regularly, this book also lists worldwide providers. For ordering information about the book and other information sources, see the appendix.

There it is. Now you know what you need to get connected to the Internet and to begin to use some of its vast resources. Our only advice is this: Keep trying when you're frustrated, keep looking when you can't find it, and keep your sense of humor. You probably couldn't ride a bicycle perfectly the first time you tried either!

The world of the Internet is immense and so, too, is the body of information about it! Our biggest task in writing this book was to sort out what you, the new Internet user, most needed to know to get started. The listing of resources that follows in the appendix is the most fitting conclusion to this book, because it gives you places to look for even more information. And we hope we've whetted your appetite for further exploration! We've given you the map, the rules of the road, and the keys to the kingdom. Enjoy your Internet journey!

Bibliography

Adams, Rick, and Brian Reid. "USENET Readership Summary Report for March 1992," *Internet Society News*, vol. 1, no. 2, pp. 40–41. Reston, Va.: Internet Society, spring 1992.

Barlow, John Perry. "Crime and Puzzlement: Desperados of the DataSphere," *Whole Earth Review*, pp. 45–57. Sausalito, Calif.: POINT, fall 1990.

Barron, Billy. *UNT's Accessing On-Line Bibliographic Databases*. Denton, Tex.: University of North Texas, April 24, 1992.

Berners-Lee, Tim. "A Summary of the WorldWideWeb System," *ConneXions: The Interoperability Report*, vol. 6, no. 7, pp. 26–27. Mountain View, Calif.: Interop Company, July 1992.

Berners-Lee, Tim, Robert Cailliau, Jean-Fracois Groff, and Bernd Pollermann. "World-Wide Web: The Information Universe," *Electronic Networking: Research, Applications and Policy*, vol. 2, no. 1, pp. 52–58. Westport, Conn.: Meckler Corporation, spring 1992.

Bonine, John E. "Internet and Environmental Law," *Internet Society News*, vol. 1, no. 1, pp. 26–27. Reston, Va.: Internet Society, winter 1992.

Bromberg, Craig. "In Defense of Hackers," *The New York Times Magazine*, pp. 44–49. New York: The New York Times, April 21, 1991.

Cerf, Vinton G. "The Internet Activities Board; RFC 1120," *Network Working Group Request for Comments*. May 1990.

Cerf, Vinton G. "Networks," *Scientific American*, vol. 265, no. 3, pp. 72–81. New York: Scientific American, Inc., September 1991.

Chew, John J. *Inter-Network Mail Guide*. June 25, 1992.

Clements, Charles, M.D. "HealthNet Connects Africa to Vital Medical Data," *Satellite Communications*, pp. 18–21. January 1992.

Comer, Douglas E. *Internetworking with TCP/IP: Principles, Protocols and Architecture*, Second Edition, Vol. 1. Englewood Cliffs, N.J.: Prentice Hall, 1991.

Curry, David A. *Improving the Security of Your UNIX System*. Menlo Park, Calif.: SRI International Information and Telecommunications Sciences and Technology Division, April 1990.

Denning, Peter J. *Computers Under Attack: Intruders, Worms and Viruses*. Reading, Mass.: Addison-Wesley, 1990.

Deutsch, Peter. "Resource Discovery in an Internet Environment—the Archie Approach," *Electronic Networking: Research, Applications, and Policy*, vol. 2, no. 1, pp. 45–51. Westport, Conn.: Meckler Corporation, spring 1992.

Emtage, Alan, Brewster Kahle, B. Clifford Neuman, and Michael Schwartz. *A Comparison of Internet Resource Discovery Approaches*. Boulder, Colo.: University of Colorado at Boulder Department of Computer Science, July 1992.

Goos, Anke, and Daniel Karrenberg. *The European R&D E-Mail Directory*. Buntingford, United Kingdom: EurOpen, 1990.

Gore, Al. "Infrastructure for the Global Village," *Scientific American*, vol. 265, no. 3, pp. 150–153. New York: Scientific American, Inc., September 1991.

Holbrook, Paul, and Joyce K. Reynolds. "Site Security Handbook; RFC 1244 or FYI 8, " *Network Working Group Request for Comments*. July 1991.

Horvitz, Robert. "The USENET Underground," *Whole Earth Review*, no. 65, pp. 112–115. Sausalito, Calif.: POINT, winter 1989.

Kahle, Brewster. "WAIS: Wide Area Information Servers," *NSF Network News*, no. 11, pp. 1–2. Cambridge, Mass.: The NSF Network Service Center, March 1992.

Kaminski, Peter. "Public Dialup Internet Access List," *alt.internet.access.wanted*. USENET, August 25, 1992.

Kamens, Jonathan. "How to Find Sources," *news.answers*. USENET, August 15, 1992.

Kapor, Mitchell. "Civil Liberties in Cyberspace," *Scientific American*, vol. 265, no. 3, pp. 158–164. New York: Scientific American, Inc., September 1991.

Karraker, Roger. "Highways of the Mind," *Whole Earth Review*, no. 70, pp. 4–11. Sausalito, Calif.: POINT, spring 1991.

Kehoe, Brendan, P. *Zen and the Art of the Internet: A Beginner's Guide to the Internet.* Chester, Pa.: Widener University, January 1992.

Kochmer, Jonathan. *NorthWestNet User Services Internet Resource Guide (NUSIRG).* Bellevue, Wash.: NorthWestNet and NorthWestNet Academic Computing Consortium, Inc., December 1991.

Landweber, Larry. "International Connectivity," *Internet Society News,* vol. 1, no. 2, pp. 49–52. Reston, Va.: Internet Society, spring 1992.

LaQuey, Tracy L. *The User's Directory of Computer Networks.* Burlington, Mass.: Digital Press, 1990.

Libes, Don, and Sandy Ressler. *Life with UNIX: A Guide for Everyone.* Englewood Cliffs, N.J.: Prentice Hall, 1989.

Lottor, Mark. "Internet Growth (1981–1991); RFC 1296," *Network Working Group Request for Comments.* January 1992.

Malkin, Gary, and April Marine. "FYI on Questions and Answers: Answers to Commonly Asked New Internet User Questions; RFC 1325 or FYI 4," *Network Working Group Request for Comments.* May 1992.

Marine, April (Editor), Susan Kirkpatrick, Vivan Neou, and Carol Ward. *Internet: Getting Started.* Menlo Park, Calif.: SRI International, May 1992.

MaCahill, Mark. "The Internet Gopher: A Distributed Server Information System," *ConneXions: The Interoperability Report,* vol. 6, no. 7, pp. 10–14. Mountain View, Calif: Interop Company, July 1992.

McClure, Charles R., Ann P. Bishop, Philip Doty, and Howard Rosenbaum. *The National Research and Education Network (NREN): Research and Policy Perspectives.* Norwood, N.J.: Ablex Publishing Corporation, 1991.

Mockapetris, Paul. "Domain Names—Concepts and Facilities; RFC 822," *Network Working Group Request for Comments.* November 1983.

Moore, Michael A., and Ronald M. Sawey. *BITNET for VMS Users.* Burlington, Mass.: Digital Press, 1992.

O'Brien, Michael. "Ask Mr. Protocol—Playing in the MUD," *SunExpert,* vol. 3, no. 5, pp. 19–27. Brookline, Mass.: Computer Publishing Group, May 1992.

Press, Larry. "Relcom, An Appropriate Technology Network," *INET '92 Proceedings, Kobe, Japan*. Reston, Va.: Internet Society, June 1992.

Quarterman, John S. *The Matrix: Computer Networks and Conferencing Systems Worldwide*. Burlington, Mass.: Digital Press, 1990.

Quarterman, John S. "Which Network and Why It Matters," *Matrix News*, vol. 1, no. 5, pp. 6–13. Austin, Tex.: Matrix Information and Directory Services, Inc., August 1991.

Quarterman, John S. "Analogy is Not Identity," *Matrix News*, vol. 1, no. 7, pp. 6–9. Austin, Tex.: Matrix Information and Directory Services, Inc., October 1991.

Raymond, Eric, and Guy L. Steele Jr. *The New Hacker's Dictionary*. Cambridge, Mass.: The MIT Press, 1992.

Salzenberg, Chip. "What is Usenet?" *news.announce.newusers*. USENET, July 19, 1992.

Spafford, Gene. "Do Not Send Any {Get Well, Post, Business} Cards to Craig Shergold," *news.announce.important*. USENET, 1992.

Spafford, Gene. "List of Active Newsgroups," *news.announce.newusers*. USENET, July 19, 1992.

Stoll, Clifford. *The Cuckoo's Egg: Tracking a Spy Through the Maze of Computer Espionage*. New York: Doubleday, 1989.

SURAnet Network Information Center. *SURAnet Information Available on the Internet: A Guide to Selected Sources*. College Park, Md.: SURAnet, August 3, 1992.

Toffler, Alvin. *Powershift: Knowledge, Wealth, and Violence at the Edge of the 21st Century*. New York: Bantam Books, November 1990.

Weiser, Mark. "The Computer for the 21st Century," *Scientific American*, vol. 265, no. 3, pp. 94–104. New York: Scientific American, Inc., September 1991.

Wyk, Kenneth R. van. "Frequently Asked Questions on VIRUS-L/comp.virus," *VIRUS-L Digest*. *VIRUS-L@ibm1.cc.lehigh.edu*, March 19, 1992.

Yanoff, Scott. *Special Internet Connections*. Milwaukee, Wis.: University of Wisconsin, June 30. 1992.

Appendix: Resources

CLIENT SOFTWARE AND MENU SYSTEMS

Information Searching and Retrieval Clients

Archie   Archie clients can be obtained via anonymous FTP to host *quiche.cs.mcgill.ca*, directory *archie/clients*. Get the *README* file for more information. Send questions about archie to *archie-l@archie.mcgill.ca*.

WAIS   The main distribution site for WAIS software is on host *think.com*, directory *wais*. Get the file *README* for more information. Send comments and questions about WAIS to Brewster Kahle, *brewster@think.com*.

Gopher   Obtain Gopher clients via anonymous FTP to host *boombox.micro.umn.edu*, in the *pub/gopher* directory. See the *00README* file for more information. Send suggestions and comments about Gopher to *gopher@boombox.micro.umn.edu*.

WorldWideWeb   The main software distribution site for WWW software is on the anonymous FTP host *info.cern.ch*, directory *pub/WWW*; get the *README.txt* file. Send WWW comments and questions to Tim Berners-Lee, *timbl@info.cern.ch*.

Menu-Based Systems

The menu systems that organize and enable access to online library catalogs, databases, BBSs, and CWIS include HYTELNET, as well as LIBTEL and CATALIST. These programs and others can be also be obtained via anonymous FTP on host *ftp.unt.edu*, directory *library*.

CATALIST   Developed by Richard Duggan, University of Delaware, Newark, Del. CATALIST requires MicroSoft Windows 3.0 to run. It's available via anonymous FTP on *zebra.acs.udel.edu*, directory *pub/library*. Get the file *readme.txt* for more information.

Hytelnet   Developed by Peter Scott, University of Saskatchewan, Saskatoon, Canada. Hytelnet programs for PC, Mac, VMS
and UNIX are available on host *access.usask.ca*, directory
pub/hytelnet. Get the *README* file for more information.

LIBTEL   Developed by Dan Mahone, University of New Mexico, Albuquerque, N.M. UNIX and VMS versions are available
via anonymous FTP on host *ftp.unt.edu*, directory *library*. See
the *libtel* files.

COMMERCIAL NETWORKING

Trade Association of Commercial Internet Providers
The Commercial Internet Exchange (CIX) Association
Phone: (617) 864-0665
Email: *info@cix.org*
Anonymous FTP: *cix.org*. See the *cix- info.txt* file.

Enterprise Networking
Enterprise Integration Networking (EINet)
Microelectronics and Computer Technology Corporation (MCC)
3500 West Balcones Center Drive, Austin, TX 78759
Phone: (512) 338-3569   FAX: (512) 338-3897
Email: *info@einet.net*   Email server: *einet-info@einet.net*
Anonymous FTP: *ftp.einet.net*

Commercial Information Services
Dialog Information Services
Phone: (415) 858-3785, (800) 3-DIALOG   FAX: (415) 858-7069
Dow Jones News/Retrieval, Dow Jones Information Services
Phone: (800) 522-3567, (609) 452-1511

Lexis-Nexis, Mead Data Central, Inc.
Phone: (800) 227-4908

ClariNet Communications Corporation
Phone: (408) 296-0366, (800) USE-NETS   FAX: (408) 296-1668
Email: *info@clarinet.com*   Anonymous FTP: *ftp.clarinet.com*

DIRECTORY SERVICES

Documents
How to Find People's E-Mail Addresses FAQ, by Jonathan Kamens,
Massachusetts Institute of Technology, Cambridge, Mass. Available via anonymous FTP on host *pit-manager.mit.edu*, directory
pub/usenet/news.answers, filename *finding-addresses*.

List of Internet Whois Servers, by Matt Power, Massachusetts Institute of Technology, Cambridge, Mass. Available via anonymous FTP on host *sipb.mit.edu*, directory *pub/whois*, filename *whois-servers.list*.

INTEREST GROUPS AND PROFESSIONAL ORGANIZATIONS

Federation of Academic and Research Networks
FARNET, Attn: Laura Breeden
100 Fifth Avenue, Waltham, MA 02154
Phone: (617) 890-5120   FAX: (617) 890-5117
Email: *breeden@farnet.org*   Anonymous FTP: *farnet.org*

K–12 Networking
Consortium for School Networking (CoSN)
P.O. Box 65193, Washington, DC 20035–5193
Phone: (202) 466-6296
Email: *cosn@bitnic.bitnet*

Library Networking
Coalition for Networked Information (CNI)
1527 New Hampshire Avenue, NW, Washington, DC 20036
Phone: (202) 232-2466   FAX: (202) 462-7849
Email: *info@cni.org*   Anonymous FTP: *ftp.cni.org*

Public Access Computer Systems List (PACS-L). Moderated by Charles Bailey.
LISTSERV Address: *LISTSERV@UHUPVM1.bitnet*.
List Address: PACS-L@UHUPVM1.bitnet.

INTERNET AND ACADEMIC AND RESEARCH NETWORKS
Books

Frey, Donnalyn, and Rick Adams. *!%@:: A Directory of Electronic Mail Addressing and Networks*. Sebastopol, Calif.: O'Reilly & Associates, Inc., 1990.

Krol, Ed. *The Whole Internet User's Guide and Catalog*. Sebastopol, Calif.: O'Reilly & Associates, Inc., 1992.

LaQuey, Tracy L. *The User's Directory of Computer Networks*. Burlington, Mass.: Digital Press, 1990.

Malamud, Carl. *Exploring the Internet: A Technical Travelogue*. Englewood Cliffs, N.J.: Prentice Hall, 1992.

Quarterman, John S. *The Matrix: Computer Networks and Conferencing Systems Worldwide*. Burlington, Mass.: Digital Press, 1990.

Tennant, Roy, John Ober, and Anne G. Lipow. *Crossing the Internet Threshold: An Instructional Handbook*. Berkeley, Calif.: Library Solutions Institute and Press, 1992.

Email List

INFO-NETS@THINK.COM   This mailing list is for general discussion of networks, focusing on internetwork connectivity. Focuses on general worldwide networking questions, connections to particular sites, and announcements of new networks and services. Archives are maintained and can be accessed via anonymous FTP to *think.com*, directory *mail*. All subscription requests should be sent to *info-nets-request@think.com*.

Journals and Newsletters

Electronic Networking: Research, Applications, and Policy
Meckler Corporation
11 Ferry Lane West, Westport, CT 06880
Phone: (203) 226-6967
Email: *meckler@jvnc.net*

Matrix News
Matrix Information & Directory Services, Inc. (MIDS)
P.O. Box 14621
Austin, TX 78761
Phone: (512) 329-1087   FAX: (512) 327-1274
Email: *mids@tic.com*

Research & Education Networking
Meckler Corporation
11 Ferry Lane West, Westport, CT 06880
Phone: (203) 226-6967
Email: *meckler@jvnc.net*

Lists & Guides for Online Library Catalogs, BBSs, and Databases

University of North Texas' Accessing On-line Bibliography Databases, by Billy Barron, University of North Texas, Denton, Tex. Directory of online library catalogs and databases. Available via anonymous FTP on *ftp.unt.edu*, directory *library*. There are several formats (PostScript, text, WordPerfect) of this document available. Look at the *libraries* files.

Internet—Accessible Library Catalogs & Databases. by Art St. George, University of New Mexico, and Ron Larsen, University of Maryland. Directory of online library catalogs and databases.

Available via anonymous FTP on *ariel.unm.edu* in the *library* directory. Text version is filename *internet.library*. Postscript version is *library.ps*.

Internet Resource Guide, by the NSF Network Service Center (NNSC), BBN Laboratories, Inc., Cambridge, Mass. Available via anonymous FTP on *nnsc.nsf.net*, directory *resource-guide*. Get the *README* file for instructions on getting the guide. Contact the NNSC for more information (address below).

SURAnet Information Available on the Internet: A Guide to Selected Sources, by the SURAnet Network Information Center, College Park, Md. This is a weekly updated guide to new and unique Internet resources. Available via anonymous FTP on *ftp.sura.net*, directory *pub/nic*. Filename is *infoguide.x-xx.txt*, where *x-xx* is the prefix for the most current dated version. For more information, get the *00- README.FIRST* file.

Special Internet Connections, compiled by Scott Yanoff, University of Wisconsin, Milwaukee, Wis. Posted regularly to the USENET *alt.internet.services* newsgroup. Also available via anonymous FTP on *csd4.csd.uwm.edu*, directory *pub*, filename *inet.services.txt*.

Campus-Wide Information Systems (CWIS), compiled by Judy Hallman, University of North Carolina, Chapel Hill, N.C. Available via anonymous FTP on *ftp.oit.unc.edu*, directory *pub/docs*, filename *cwis-l*.

Lists of Electronic Mail Gateways and Interest Groups
Inter-Network Mail Guide, by John J. Chew, University of Toronto, Toronto, Canada. Posted regularly to the USENET *comp.mail.misc* and *news.newusers.questions* newsgroups. Available via anonymous FTP to *FTP.MsState.Edu*, directory *pub/docs*, filename *internetwork-mail-guide*. Also available via email by sending a message to *listserv@unmvm.bitnet* with the command **get network guide** in the body.

List of Interest Groups, compiled and maintained at SRI International Network Information Systems Center, Menlo Park, Calif. Available via anonymous FTP on *ftp.nisc.sri.com*, directory *netinfo*, filename *interest-groups*.

List of BITNET LISTSERV Lists, compiled and maintained at the BITNET Network Information Center (BITNIC), Washington,

DC. Available via email by sending a message to
listserv@bitnic.bitnet. In the body of the message type the command **list global.** For more information, contact the BITNIC,
1112 Sixteenth Street, NW, Washington, DC 20036. Phone:
(202) 872-4200. Email: *info@bitnic.educom.edu*.

Directory of Scholarly Electronic Conferences, compiled by Diane K.
Kovacs, Kent State University Libraries, Kent, Ohio. Available
via anonymous FTP on host *ksuvxa.kent.edu*, directory *library*.
Get the *ACADLIST.README* file for more information.

Publicly Accessible Mailing Lists, compiled and maintained
by Stephanie da Silva, originally by Chuq Von Ruspach.
Posted regularly to USENET newsgroups, *news.lists*,
news.announce.newusers, *news.answers*. Also available via anonymous FTP on host *pit-manager.mit.edu*, directory
pub/usenet/news.answers/mailing-lists, filenames *part1*, *part2*, and
part3.

Lists and Guides for Finding Information and Software Sources
List of Anonymous FTP Sites, by Tom Czarnik. Posted regularly
to USENET newsgroups *comp.misc*, *news.answers*,
comp.sources.wanted, and *alt.sources.wanted*. Also available
in multipart files via anonymous FTP on host
pit-manager.mit.edu, directory *pub/usenet/comp.misc*.

How to Find Sources and List of Mail Servers, by Jonathan Kamens,
Massachusetts Institute of Technology, Cambridge, Mass.
Includes a list of anonymous FTP sites that allow files to be
accessed via email. Available via anonymous FTP on host
pit-manager.mit.edu, directory *pub/usenet/news.answers*, filename
finding-sources. This file is also available via an email server. For
directions, send a message to *mail-server@pit- manager.mit.edu*,
with the command **help** in the Subject.

Hypercard Tours of the Internet
Tour of the Internet. Developed by the NSF Network Service Center (NNSC), BBN Laboratories, Inc., Cambridge, Mass. Available via anonymous FTP on host *nnsc.nsf.net*, directory
internet-tour. Get the *Internet-Tour-README* file for instructions
on getting and installing this HyperCard stack. Contact the
NNSC for more information (address below).

A Cruise of the Internet. Developed by Merit Network, Inc., Ann Arbor, Mich. Available via anonymous FTP on host *nic.merit.edu*, directory *resources*. See the file *merit.cruise.readme.txt* for more information. Contact Merit Network, Inc., 1075 Beal Avenue, Ann Arbor, Mich. 48109–2112. Email address: *nsfnet-info@merit.edu*.

Online Documents and Books

For Your Information (FYI) Documents are available via anonymous FTP on host *nic.ddn.mil* in the *rfc* directory. Get the *fyi-index.txt* file for more information. See the "Internetworking and TCP/IP Resources" section in this appendix for more information about obtaining FYI/RFCs.

Zen and the Art of the Internet, by Brendan Kehoe, Widener University, Chester, Pa. Available online via anonymous FTP on *ftp.cs.widener.edu*, directory *pub/zen*. See the *README* file for more information.

NorthWestNet User Services Internet Resource Guide (NUSIRG), by Jonathan Kochmer, University of Washington, Seattle, WA. Available online in PostScript form on host *ftphost.nwnet.net*, directory *nic/nwnet/user-guide*. Get the *README.nusirg* file for more information. Also available in hard copy. Contact NorthWestNet, NUSIRG Orders, 15400 SE 30th Place, Suite 202, Bellevue, WA 98007. Phone: (206) 562-3000. Email: *nusirg-orders@nwnet.net*.

Periodic Postings and Frequently Asked Questions (FAQs) Lists and Archives

USENET FAQs   Posted or emailed regularly to newsgroups and mailing lists. USENET FAQs are also regularly posted on the USENET newsgroup *news.answers*. FAQs also archived and available via anonymous FTP on host *pit-manager.mit.edu*, directory *pub/usenet/news.answers*. For more information, see the *introduction* file in the *news-answers* directory.

Periodic Postings   Compiled and maintained by Jonathan I. Kamens, Massachusetts Institute of Technology, Cambridge, Mass. (originally by Rich Kulawiec). Periodic documents are posted or emailed regularly to newsgroups and mailing lists. List of USENET periodic postings available from host *pit-manager.mit.edu*, directory *pub/usenet/news.answers/periodic-postings*, filenames *part1, part2, part3*. Actual documents are available via anonymous FTP, host *pit-manager.mit.edu*, directory *pub/usenet*. Documents are organized by newsgroup directories. Type the file names *exactly* as shown.

NETWORK INFORMATION CENTERS (NICs)

Defense Data Network (DDN) Network Information Center (NIC)
Government Systems, Inc., Attn: Network Information Center
14200 Park Meadow Drive, Suite 200, Chantilly, VA 22021
Phone: (703) 802-4535, (800) 365-3642   FAX: (703) 802-8376
Email: *hostmaster@nic.ddn.mil*   Anonymous FTP: *nic.ddn.mil*

NSF Network Service Center
BBN Systems and Technologies Corporation
10 Moulton Street, Cambridge, MA 02138
Phone: (617) 873-3400   FAX: (617) 873-5620
Email: *nnsc@nnsc.nsf.net*   Anonymous FTP: *nnsc.nsf.net*

SRI International, Network Information Systems Center
333 Ravenswood Avenue, Menlo Park, CA 94025
Phone: (415) 859-6387   FAX: (415) 859-6028
Email: *nisc@nisc.sri.com*   Anonymous FTP: *ftp.nisc.sri.com*

NATIONAL RESEARCH AND EDUCATION NETWORK (NREN)

Books

Kahin, Brian. *Building Information Infrastructure: Issues in the Development of the National Research and Education Network (NREN)*. New York: McGraw-Hill, 1992.

McClure, Charles R., Ann P. Bishop, Philip Doty, and Howard Rosenbaum. *The National Research and Education Network (NREN): Research and Policy Perspectives*. Norwood, N.J.: Ablex Press, 1991.

Parkhurst, Carol A. *Library Perspectives on NREN: The National Research and Education Network*. Chicago, Ill.: Library and Information Technology Association (LITA), a division of the American Library Association, 1990.

Online Documents

Thoughts on the National Research and Education Network, by Vinton G. Cerf, Corporation for National R, Reston, Va. Available via anonymous FTP on host *nic.ddn.mil, directory rfc,* filename *rfc1167.txt.*

Libraries and the National Research and Education Network, available via anonymous FTP on host *ftp.eff.org*, directory *pub/internet-info*, filename *lita.nren*.

NREN Legislation and Remarks, available via anonymous FTP on host *ftp.merit.edu*, directory *internet/legislative.actions*. See the *INDEX.legislative.actions* file for more information.

ELECTRONIC FRONTIER

Organizations
Electronic Frontier Foundation (EFF)
The Electronic Frontier Foundation, Inc.
155 Second Street, Cambridge, MA 02141
Phone: (617) 864-0665   FAX: (617) 864-0866

The Electronic Frontier Foundation, Inc.
666 Pennsylvania Avenue, S.E., Suite 303
Washington, DC 20003
Phone: (202) 544-9237   FAX: (202) 547-5481
Email: *eff@eff.org*   Anonymous FTP: *ftp.eff.org*
USENET Newsgroups: *comp.org.eff.talk* and *comp.org.eff.news*

Books
Hafner, Katie, and John Markoff. *Cyberpunk: Outlaws and Hackers on the Computer Frontier*. New York: Simon & Schuster, 1991.

Raymond, Eric, and Guy L. Steele Jr. *The New Hacker's Dictionary*. Cambridge, Mass.: The MIT Press, 1992.

Sterling, Bruce. *The Hacker Crackdown: Law and Disorder on the Electronic Frontier*. New York: Bantam Books, 1992.

Stoll, Clifford. *The Cuckoo's Egg: Tracking a Spy Through the Maze of Computer Esponiage*. New York: Doubleday, 1989.

INTERNET ORGANIZATIONAL AND INDIVIDUAL ACCESS PROVIDERS

National Commercial Internet Providers
Advanced Network & Services, Inc. (ANS) and ANS CO+RE
100 Clearbrook Road, Elmsford, NY 10523
Phone: (914) 789-5300   FAX: (914) 789-5310
Email: *info@ans.net*   Anonymous FTP: *ftp.ans.net*

California Education & Research Federation Network (CERFnet)
P.O. Box 85608, San Diego, CA 92186–9784
Phone: (619) 455-3900, (800) 876- 2373   FAX: (619) 455-3990
Email: *help@cerf.net*   Anonymous FTP: *nic.cerf.net*

Sprint
Bob Doyle, Sprintlink
13221 Woodland Park Road, Herndon, VA 22071
Phone: (703) 904-2167   FAX: (703) 904-2680
Email: *bdoyle@icml.icp.net*

Performance Systems International, Inc. (PSI)
11800 Sunrise Valley Drive, Suite 1100, Reston, VA 22091
Phone: (703) 620-6651, (800) 82-PSI- 82   FAX: (703) 620-4586
Email: *info@psi.com*   Email server: *all-info@psi.com*
Anonymous FTP: *ftp.psi.com*

UUNET Technologies, Inc.
3110 Fairview Park Drive, Suite 570, Falls Church, VA 22042
Phone: (703) 204-8000, (800) 4-UUNET-3   FAX: (703) 204-8001
Email: *alternet-info@uunet.uu.net*

Radiomail
Anterior Technology
P.O. Box 1206, Menlo Park, CA 94026–1206
Phone: (415) 322-1753   FAX: (415) 328-5615
Email: *support@fernwood.mpk.ca.us*
Email Server: *info@fernwood.mpk.ca.us*

PUBLIC ACCESS SYSTEMS (INDIVIDUAL ACCESS)

Source: Most of the following information and provider listing
was obtained from *Public Dialup Internet Access List (PDIAL)*, compiled by Peter Kaminski and used with permission. Send additions and corrections to *kaminski@netcom.com*. See the "Lists of
Providers" section in this appendix for information on obtaining the latest online list.

Many of these systems run the UNIX operating system. All
provide dialup terminal emulation. Ask about UUCP, SLIP, or
PPP access. Typical services include USENET, IRC, BBS, and
games. Most of these systems offer local area dialup access. (See
the "Dialup" field for the local modem number and a new user
login name, if one exists.) A summary of services by area code is
provided. (See "Local Dialup Access Providers Summary.")

A good number of systems also provide access for users outside their local areas. (See the "Wide Area Access Providers
Summary" section.) Wide area access is usually offered via a
public data network (PDN, contact information listed below)

and is specified in the "Long Distance" field. "800" means the provider is accessible via a "toll-free" US phone number. The phone company will not charge for the call, but the service provider will add a relatively large surcharge to cover the high cost of the 800 service. Please note that prices, access, and services for each of these may change; use the prices listed here for guidance only and not as the definitive pricing structure for each organization.

Wide Area Access Providers Summary (offering access for most area codes in continental U.S.)

Dial-n-CERF-USA	OARnet
Holonet	Portal
Michnet	PSI
Intercon	Well
JvNC	World

Local Dialup Access Area Code Summary

201	JvNC-Tiger	510	Dial-n-CERF, Holonet, Netcom
202	Express	513	OARnet
203	JvNC-Tiger	516	JvNC-Tiger
206	Halcyon	517	MichNet
212	Panix	603	NEARnet
213	Dial-n-CERF, Netcom	609	JvNC-Tiger
215	JvNC-Tiger	614	OARnet
216	OARnet	616	MichNet
301	Express	617	NEARnet, World
303	CSN	619	Cyber, Dial-n-CERF
310	Dial-n-CERF, Netcom	703	Express
313	MichNet, MSEN	714	Dial-n-CERF
401	Anomaly, IDS, JvNC-Tiger	718	Panix
		719	CNS, CSN
408	a2i, Netcom, Portal	818	Dial-n-CERF, Netcom
410	Express	906	MichNet
415	Netcom, Well	908	JvNC-Tiger
419	OARnet	919	CONCERT
508	Nearnet		

Local Dialup Access Providers

a2i communications
1211 Park Avenue, Suite 202, San Jose, CA 95126

Phone: n/a

Email: *info@rahul.net*

Anonymous FTP: *ftp.rahul.net*, directory *pub*, filename *BLURB*

Dialup: (408) 293-9010 (v.32, v.32 bis) or (408) 293-9020 (PEP); Login as **guest**

Area Code: 408   Long Distance: Internet or PDN

Fees: $20/month, $45/3 months, or $72/6 months

Anomaly—Rhode Island's Gateway To The Internet
Small Business Systems, Inc.

Box 17220, Route 104, Smithfield, RI 02917

Phone: (401) 273-4669   FAX: (401) 823-1447

Email: *root@anomaly.sbs.risc.net*

Dialup: (401) 331-3706 (v.32) or (401) 455-0347 (PEP)

Area Code: 401   Long Distance: Internet or PDN

Fees: $125/6 months or $200/year

Colorado SuperNet, Inc. (CSN), Colorado School of Mines
1500 Illinois, Golden, CO 80401

Phone: (303) 273-3471   FAX: (303) 273-3475

Email: *info@csn.org*

Anonymous FTP: *csn.org*, directory *CSN/reports*, filename *DialinInfo.txt*

Dialup: Contact for number

Area Codes: 303, 719   Long Distance: Internet or PDN; Note: CSN serves Colorado only.

Fees: $1/hour off-peak, $2/hour peak ($250 max/month) + $20 signup

Off Peak: midnight to 6 a.m.

Community News Service
1715 Monterey Road, Colorado Springs, CO 80910

Phone: (719) 579-9120

Email: *klaus@cscns.com*

Dialup: (719) 520-1700; Login as **new**

Area Code: 719   Long Distance: Internet or PDN

Fees: $1/hour; $10/month minimum + $35 signup

CONCERT
Communications for North Carolina Education, Research, and Technology

3021 Cornwallis Road, Research Triangle Park, NC 27709

Phone: (919) 248-1999   FAX: (919) 248-1405
Email: *info@concert.net*
Dialup: Contact for number
Area Code: 919   Long Distance: Internet or PDN
Fees: $30/month + $100 signup

The Cyberspace Station
204 N. El Camino Real, Suite E626, Encinitas, CA 92024
Email: *help@cyber.net*
Dialup: (619) 634-1376, Login as **guest**
Area Code: 619   Long Distance: Internet or PDN
Fees: $15/month + $10 startup or $60 for six months

Dial n' CERF, AYC, and Dial n' CERF USA
P.O. Box 85608, San Diego, CA 92186–9784
Phone: (619) 455-3900, (800) 876-2373   FAX: (619) 455-3990
Email: *help@cerf.net*
Anonymous FTP: *nic.cerf.net*, directory *cerfnet/dial-n-cerf*
Dialup: Contact for number
Area Codes: 213, 310, 510, 619, 714, 818, 800
Long Distance: Internet, PDN, or included
Fees: ACY: $5/hour ($3/hour on weekend) + $20/month +
    $50 startup or $250/month; Dial n' CERF USA: $10/hour
    ($8/hour on weekend) + $20/month
Off Peak: Weekend: 5 p.m. Friday to 5 p.m. Sunday

Express Access—Online Communications Service
6006 Greenbelt Road #228, Greenbelt, MD 20770
Phone: (301) 220-2020
Email: *info@digex.com*
Dialup: (301) 220-0462, (410) 766-1855. Login as **new.**
Area Codes: 202, 301, 410, 703   Long Distance: Internet or PDN
Fees: $25/month or $250/year

Halcyon
P.O. Box 555, Grapeview, WA 98546
Phone: (206) 426-9298
Email: *info@halcyon.com*
Anonymous FTP: *halcyon.com*, directory *pub/waffle*, filename *info*
Dialup: (206) 382-6245; Login as **BBS**
Area Code: 206   Long Distance: Internet or PDN

HoloNet, Information Access Technologies, Inc.
46 Shattuck Square, Suite 11, Berkeley, CA 94704–1152
Phone: (510) 704-0160
FAX: 510-704-8019
Email: *info@holonet.net*
Anonymous FTP: *holonet.net*, directory *info*
Dialup: (510) 704-1058 (local only). (For demo, call 800-NET-HOLO)
Area Codes: 510, PDN   Long Distance: [per hour, off-peak/peak] Bay Area: $0.50/$0.95; PSINet A: $0.95/$1.95; PSINet B: $2.50/$6.00; Tymnet: $3.75/$7.50
Fees: $2/hour off-peak, $4/hour peak; $6/month or $60/year minimum
Off Peak: 5 p.m. to 8 a.m. + weekends and holidays

The IDS World Network, InteleCom Data Systems
11 Franklin Rd., East Greenwich, RI 02818
Phone: (401) 884-7856
Email: *sysadmin@ids.net*   Anonymous FTP: *ids.net*, filename *ids.net*
Dialup: (401) 884-9002, (401) 785-1067
Area Code: 401   Long Distance: Internet or PDN
Fees: $10/month, $50/half year, or $100/year

InterCon Systems Corporation
950 Herndon Parkway, Suite 420, Herndon, VA 22070
Phone: (703) 709-9890, (800) NET-2-YOU
FAX: (703) 709-9896
Email: *comment@intercon.com*
Dialup: Send email to *numbers- info@psi.com*
Area Code: PDN   Long Distance: included
Fees: Worldlink: $20/month + $19 startup

The John von Neumann Computer Network
Dialin' Tiger and Tiger Mail & Dialin' Terminal
JvNCnet-Princeton University
B6 von Neumann Hall, Princeton, NJ 08544
Phone: (800) 35-TIGER, (609) 258-2400
Email: *info@jvnc.net*
Dialup: Contact for number
Area Codes: 201, 203, 215, 401, 516, 609, 908, and 800

Long Distance: Internet, PDN, or included

Fees: Dialin' Tiger: $99/month + $99 startup; Tiger Mail &
Dialin' Terminal: $19/month + $10/hour + $36 startup

Merit Network, Inc.—MichNet project
University of Michigan, Institute of Science and Technology
2200 Bonisteel Avenue, Ann Arbor, MI 48109
Phone: (313) 764-9430
Email: *info@merit.edu*   Anonymous FTP: *nic.merit.edu*
Dialup: Contact for number
Area Codes: 313, 517, 616, 906, PDN
Long Distance: SprintNet, Autonet, Michigan Bell packet-
switch network
Fees: $35/month + $40 signup

MSEN, Inc.
628 Brooks St., Ann Arbor, MI 48103
Phone: (313) 998-4562   FAX: (313) 998-4563
Email: *info@msen.com*
Anonymous FTP: *ftp.msen.com* directory *pub/vendor/msen*
Dialup: (313) 998-4555. Login as **newuser.**
Area Code: 313   Long Distance: Internet or PDN
Fees: $5/month + $2/hr or $20/mo for 20 hr

NEARnet
10 Moulton Street, Cambridge, MA 02138
Phone: (617) 873-8730
Email: *nearnet-join@nic.near.net*
Anonymous FTP: *nic.near.net* directory *docs*
Dialup: Contact for numbers
Area Codes: 508, 603, 617   Long Distance: Internet or PDN
Fees: $250/month

Netcom Online Communication Services, Inc.
4000 Moorpark Ave., No. 209, San Jose, CA 95117
Phone: (408) 554-UNIX   FAX: 408-241-9145
Email: *info@netcom.com*
Dialup: (310) 842-8835, (408) 241-9760, (408) 459-9851, (415)
424-0131, (510) 426-6860, (510) 865- 9004, Login as **guest**
Area Codes: 213, 310, 408, 415, 510, 818
Long Distance: Internet or PDN
Fees: $19.50/month + $15.00 signup

OARnet, Ohio Supercomputer Center
1224 Kinnear Road, Columbus, OH 43212–1154
Phone: (614) 292-8100
Email: *nic@oar.net*
Dialup: Send email to *nic@oar.net*
Area Codes: 614, 513, 419, 216, 800
Long Distance: 800 service
Fees: $4.00/hr to $330.00/month

PANIX Public Accss Unix
Panix Public Access Unix of New York
c/o Alexis Rosen, 110 Riverside Drive, New York, NY 10024
Phone: (212) 877-4854 (Alexis Rosen), (718) 965-3768 (Jim
  Baumbach)
Email: *alexis@panix.com, jsb@panix.com*
Dialup: (718) 832-1525, Login as **newuser**
Area Codes: 212, 718   Long Distance: Internet or PDN
Fees: $19/month or $208/year + $40 signup

Performance Systems International, Inc. (PSI)
Global Dialup Service (GDS) and Personal Internet Access
  (PSILink)
11800 Sunrise Valley Drive, Suite 1100, Reston, VA 22091
Phone: (703) 620-6651, (800) 82 PSI 82   FAX: (703) 620-4586
Email: *all-info@psi.com, gds-info@psi.com*
Anonymous FTP: *ftp.psi.com*
Dialup: Send email to *numbers-info@psi.com*
Area Code: PDN   Long Distance: included
Fees: GDS: $39/month + $39 startup, PSILink: $29/month
  + $19 startup

Portal Communications Company (PORTAL-DOM)
20863 Stevens Creek Boulevard, Suite 200
Cupertino, CA 95014
Phone: (408) 973-9111
Email: *cs@cup.portal.com*
Dialup: (408) 725-0561; Login as **new, info, help**
Area Code: 408 . Long Distance: SprintNet: $2.50/hour
  off-peak, $7-$10/hour peak; Tymnet: similar
Fees: $18.95/month + $19.95 signup
Off Peak: 6 p.m. to 7 a.m. + weekends and holidays

UK PC User Group
Email: *info@ibmpcug.co.uk*
Dialup: 44 (0)81 863 6646
Area Codes: 44 (0)81   Long Distance: Internet or PDN
Fees: GBPounds 15.50/month or 160/year + 10 startup (no
    time charges)

The Whole Earth 'Lectronic Link
The WELL (Whole Earth 'Lectronic Link)
27 Gate Five Road, Sausalito, CA 94965
Phone: (415) 332-4335   FAX: (415)-332-4927
Email: *info@well.sf.ca.us*
Dialup: (415) 332-6106; Login as **newuser**
Area Codes: 415, PDN   Long Distance: CPN: $4/hour
Fees: $15.00/month + $2.00/hr

The World, Software Tool and Die
1330 Beacon Street, Brookline, MA 02146
Phone: (617) 739-0202
Email: *office@world.std.com*
Anonymous FTP: *world.std.com*, directory *world-info*, filename
    basic.info
Dialup: (617) 739-9753; Login as **new**
Area Code: 617   Long Distance: CPN: $5.60/hour
Fees: $5.00/month + $2.00/hr or $20/month for 20 hours

Public Data Networks Contacts (PDN)
BT Tymnet
Phone: (215) 666-1770, (800) 937-2862

CompuServe Packet Network (CPN)
Phone: (800) 848-4480

PC Pursuit (Sprint)
Phone: (913) 541-1025, (800) 736-1130   FAX: (913) 541-6146

PSINet
Phone: (703) 620-6651, (800) 82-PSI-82
Email: *all-info@psi.com*

Groups Offering Internet Access
Cooperative Library Agency for Systems and Services (CLASS)
1415 Koll Circle, Suite 101, San Jose, CA 95112-4698
Phone: (408) 453-0444, (800) 488-4559   FAX: (408) 453-5379

Institute for Global Communications (IGC) (Peacenet, Econet)
18 De Boom Street, San Francisco, CA 94107
Phone: (415) 442-0220   FAX: (415) 546-1794
Email: *support@igc.apc.org*

National Public Telecomputing Network (NPTN) (Freenets)
Box 1987, Cleveland, OH 44106
Phone: (216) 368-2733   FAX: (216) 368-5436
Email: *info@nptn.org*

The Texas Education Network (TENET), The Texas Education
   Agency (TEA)
1701 N. Congress Ave., Austin, TX 78701
Phone: (512) 463-0828 X. 39091   FAX: (512) 463-9090
Email: *tea@tenet.edu*

LISTS OF PROVIDERS

Internet Access Providers   Compiled and maintained by
SRI International Network Information Systems Center
(NISC), Menlo Park, Calif. Available via anonymous FTP on
host *ftp.nisc.sri.com*, directory *netinfo*, filenames
Internet-access-providers-US.txt and
Internet-access-providers-non-US.txt. Also available in hard copy
form in the book *Internet: Getting Started*. Contact the SRI NISC
(address above) for more information.

Network Provider Referral List   Compiled and maintained
by the NSF Network Service Center (NNSC), BBN Laboratories, Inc., Cambridge, Mass. Available via anonymous FTP on
host *nnsc.nsf.net*, directory *nsfnet*, filename *referral-list*. Contact
the NNSC (address in the NIC section) for more information.

Open Access UNIX Sites: NIXPUb List   Posted regularly to
USENET comp.misc, comp.bbs.misc, and *alt.bbs* newsgroups. Available via anonymous FTP on *GVL.Unisys.COM*, directory
pub/nixpub, filenames *long* or *short*. For those with UUCP access, this file is also available via anonymous UUCP from node
name *jabber*, login *nuucp*, directory */usr/spool/uucppublic*,
filename *nixpub*, or *nixpub.short*.

Public Dialup Internet Access List (PDIAL)   Compiled
and maintained by Peter Kaminski. Posted regularly to the
following USENET Newsgroups: *alt.internet.access.wanted*,
alt.bbs.lists, and *ba.internet*. Available via anonymous FTP on

host *gvl.unisys.com*, directory *pub/pubnet*, filename *pdial*. Or send a message to *info-deli-server@netcom.com* with the Subject: Send PDIAL.

SECURITY

Books

Denning, Peter J. *Computers Under Attack: Intruders, Worms and Viruses*. Reading, Mass.: Addison-Wesley, 1990.

Garfinkel, S., and E. Spafford. *Practical UNIX Security*. Sebastopol, Calif.: O'Reilly & Associates, 1991.

Mailing Lists

RISKS@csl.sri.com   The *RISKS Digest* is a moderated discussion group on general computer security issues. To subscribe, send a message to *risks-request@csl.sri.com*.

VIRUS-L@ibm1.cc.lehigh.edu   VIRUS-L is an electronic mail discussion forum devoted to sharing information about computer viruses. To subscribe, send an email message to *LISTSERV@ibm1.cc.lehigh.edu* (note this is a LISTSERV with an Internet address) and include this command in the message body: **SUB VIRUS-L** *Your-name*.

Organization

Computer Emergency Response Team (CERT)
Software Engineering Institute, Carnegie Mellon University
4500 Fifth Avenue, Pittsburgh, PA 15213
Phone: (412) 268-7090   FAX: (412) 268-6989
Email: *cert@cert.org*   Anonymous FTP: *ftp.cert.org*

Online documents

Ethics and the Internet, by the Internet Activities Board. Available online via anonymous FTP on host *nic.ddn.mil*, directory *rfc*, filename *rfc1087.txt*.

Site Security Handbook, by Paul Holbrook, CICNet, Ann Arbor, Mich., and Joyce K. Reynolds, University of Southern California, Information Sciences Institute, Marina del Rey, Calif. Available via anonymous FTP on host *nic.ddn.mil*, directory *rfc*, filename *rfc1244.txt*. Also known as FYI 8.

Virus Information Documents: Public virus informational documents are available via anonymous FTP on host *ftp.cert.org*, directory *pub/virus-l/docs*. See the *README* file for more information.

USENET Newsgroups

comp.risks   This newsgroup is the same as *RISKS Digest*.

comp.virus   This newsgroup is the same as *VIRUS-L*.

TCP/IP AND INTERNETWORKING

Books

Comer, Douglas E. *Internetworking with TCP/IP: Principles,
    Protocols and Architecture, Second Edition, Volume 1*. Englewood
    Cliffs, N.J.: Prentice Hall, Inc., 1991.

Marine, April, Susan Kirkpatrick, Vivan Neou, and Carol Ward.
    Internet: Getting Started. Menlo Park, Calif.: SRI International,
    May 1992. See the NIC section for contact information.

Email Lists

tcp-ip@nic.ddn.mil. This mailing list is a discussion group for
TCP/IP developers and maintainers. Send subscription requests
to *tcp-ip-request@nic.ddn.mil*.

Newsletter

ConneXions: The Interoperability Report
Interop Company
480 San Antonio Road, Suite 100, Mountain View, CA 94040
Phone: (800) INTEROP, (415) 941- 3399   FAX: (415) 941-2913
Email: *connexions@interop.com*

Online Documents

Network Reading List, by Charles Spurgeon, The University of
Texas at Austin Network Information Center, Austin, Tex.
Available in PostScript and text formats via anonymous FTP on
host *ftp.utexas.edu*, directory *pub/netinfo/reading-list*.

Request For Comments (RFCs and FYIs) can be obtained via
anonymous FTP from the following hosts: *nic.ddn.mil,
ftp.nisc.sri.com, nis.nsf.net, nisc.jvnc.net, venera.isi.edu,
wuarchive.wustl.edu, src.doc.ic.ac.uk,* or *ftp.concert.net*. RFCs (and
the RFC index) can be obtained via email also. Send a message
to *rfc-info@isi.edu*, and in the body of the message put the command **help: ways_to_get_rfcs**. A help message will be returned to you. RFCs are also available in hard copy form on a
cost recovery basis from SRI International Network Information Systems Center. See the contact information in the NIC
section.

Organization

Internet Society (ISOC)
1895 Preston White Drive, Suite 100, Reston, VA 22091
Phone: (703) 648-9888   FAX: (703) 620-0913
Email: *isoc@cnri.reston.va.us*   Anonymous FTP: *cnri.reston.va.us*

UNIX

Books

Libes, Don, and Sandy Ressler. *Life with UNIX: A Guide for Everyone*. Englewood Cliffs, N.J.: Prentice Hall, 1989.

McGilton, Henry, and Rachel Morgan. *Introducing the UNIX System*. New York: McGraw- Hill, 1983.

Norton, Peter, and Harley Hahn. *Peter Norton's Guide to UNIX*. New York: Bantam Books, 1990.

Todino, Grace, and John Strang. *Learning the UNIX Operating System*. Sebastopol, Calif.: O'Reilly & Associates, Inc., 1989.

The latest version of this appendix is archived at the Online Book Store (OBS) on The World, anonymous FTP host world.std.com, directory OBS/The.Internet.Companion, filename Appendix.

Index

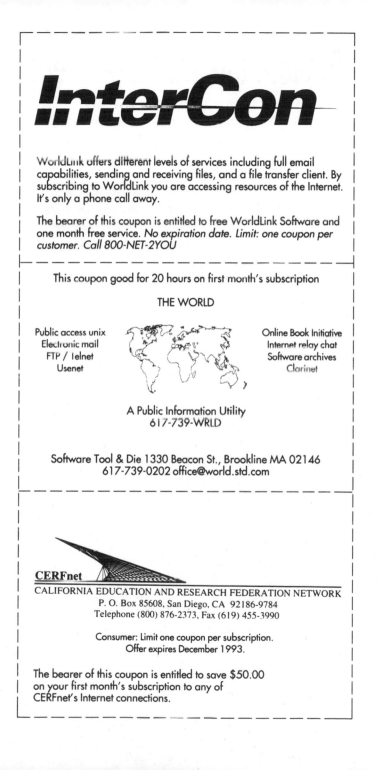

Explore the Internet – Free!

DELPHI, a leading international online service, now offers full access to the Internet. You can explore this incredible network with no risk. You get 5 hours of access to try it out for free!

 No matter where you live, DELPHI is probably just a local call away. There are access numbers in over 600 cities and towns throughout the US and many other countries.

DELPHI places a priority on helping new members learn how to use powerful Internet features such as Email, telnet, FTP, Gopher, Hytelnet, WAIS, The World-Wide Web, Internet Relay Chat, and USENET Newsgroups. There are expert online assistants and a large collection of help files, books, and other resources to help you get started.

You can use any type of computer and modem to access DELPHI. After the free trial you can choose from two low-cost membership plans. With rates as low as $1 per hour, no other online service offers so much for so little.